Christian
MANHOOD

Titles in the School of the Word series:

Christian
MANHOOD

David Matthew

Harvestime

Published in the United Kingdom by:
Harvestime Publishing Ltd, 69 Main Street
Markfield, Leicester LE6 0UT, UK

Scripture quotations are generally taken from the
New International Version. Copyright © 1978 by the New York
International Bible Society and published by
Hodder & Stoughton. Used by permission.

ISBN 0-947714-06-5

Typeset in the United Kingdom by:
ScribeTech Ltd, Bradford BD8 7BX

Printed and bound in Great Britain by
BPCC Hazell Books
Aylesbury, Bucks, England
Member of BPCC Ltd.

Increasing numbers of people are wanting to study the Word of God in depth. To go to a Bible college or seminary is not feasible for the majority, yet they desire more than the average church is able to provide in its teaching curriculum.

The book you are about to study is part of a library of components that together provide a comprehensive overview of the Scriptures in relation to life. Each book is complete in itself but is developed in such a way that the best result is experienced by studying it as part of the whole series.

We have produced the curriculum so that each component, in addition to its use as a personal study, can provide a seven-week teaching programme for study in church, home, college campus, school, military base, prison or any other group setting.

It is our prayer that you will be greatly enriched in your spiritual development through this book.

Bryn Jones
Founder — School of the Word

Getting the Most Out of This Study

This School of the Word study book is one of a series designed to relate Bible truths to everyday life. Each of the seven lessons starts with a direct search of the Scriptures and ends with a challenge to the student to apply the truths discovered. As the blank spaces left in Bible verses are filled in, the most important words and phrases stand out clearly on the page.

The material can be used in a number of different ways. It can form the basis of an individual study or be used in a group setting over a number of weeks. But experience has shown that it has the greatest benefit when a group of people study it together under a leader who is well prepared.

Tips for Leaders

If you are a leader planning to take a number of people through this study, you should consider the following:

1. Be prepared

It is essential that you do the whole study in advance yourself. This will help you to be conversant with the basic outline and have a feeling for the level of teaching based on it that your students can take.

2. Keep to the outline

It is important to keep to the outline contained in this study. This has been carefully designed to build principle on principle, 'precept upon precept' (Isaiah 28:10 RAV), with the eventual aim of the student becoming 'thoroughly equipped for every good work' (2 Timothy 3:17).

Whatever happens, don't allow your teaching to digress and become an opportunity to preach an hour's sermon!

3. Use your own experience

Even though you are staying with the outline, where possible introduce additional illustrations and applications drawn from your own experience. This makes the basic teaching more relevant to the local setting. In addition, you may wish to add more emphasis to certain points.

4. Avoid indigestion

Each lesson should take about an hour to complete. You may like to divide this into two half-hour sessions by arranging a short break for coffee and a chat halfway through. That way, the teaching is kept to manageable portions.

In some cases you may feel that the group discussion is of such vital importance to your local area that you want to spread each lesson over two weeks. If you do this, try to divide the questions at the end so that they are relevant to that week's teaching.

5. Have the right tools

Make sure that all the students have access to a copy of the New International Version of the Bible — upon which the book is based. Encourage them to fill in the blank spaces in advance but to leave answering the true/false questions until after each teaching session.

Tips for Students

Before you start the study you need to ask yourself: Am I really committed to growing as a disciple of Jesus Christ? If the answer is yes, then you're ready to proceed. Here are some immediate steps you can take to ensure maximum benefit from the course:

1. Determine your goal

This book is designed to help you achieve God's goal and destiny for you. It doesn't matter whether you are young or old, a recent convert or someone who has been a Christian for many years.

Today you are taking a step towards the fulfilment of your destiny.

Look ahead and see yourself as God desires you to be. Then confess your commitment: 'This is the kind of person I *will* become.'

2. Plan your progress

Your faith commitment to work through this book, and so take one more step towards becoming the person God intends you to be, must not only be pursued but measured in its progress. The apostle Paul said:

> *'By the grace given me I say to every one of you: Do not think of yourself more highly than you ought, but rather think of yourself with sober judgment, in accordance with the measure of faith God has given you.'*

> (Romans 12:3)

You know the kind of person you already are. You know the level of commitment you already have in your life. Now from this point determine how much time per day or week you are prepared to give to the study of the Word of God to achieve your goal.

At the end of each lesson in this study-book there is an opportunity for you to complete assignments and answer some Bible-based questions. This helps to fix the Word of God more firmly in your heart, and thus provide a reservoir of truth that the Holy Spirit can draw upon in the training of your life.

3. Recruit to the study course

Fellowship is one of the keys to Christian growth. The word 'fellowship' comes from the Greek word *koinonia*, which means to 'share things in common'.

Nothing will facilitate your progress as much as encouraging others to share in the same study programme with you, either on a personal basis or in a group. Share with each other the things you are learning and discovering in the Word of God and in life.

In this way you will be able to practise together much of what you study, and so strengthen each other in faith, just as 'iron sharpens iron' (Proverbs 27:17).

4. Set and maintain your standards

If this study is to be of maximum benefit to you, it must not be hurried. It is no use merely reading the written material and rushing the assignment. The book is designed to provoke you to your own searching and thinking, and to a demonstration of faith in God.

5. Check your progress

Once you have worked right through the book, ask your pastor or church leader to read through your answers. If he is satisfied that you have done your best to complete the questions, get him to send us a note to this effect. We will then forward a certificate for him to sign and present to you.

Your pastor is also the best person to monitor your progress and share your zeal to develop as a Christian disciple. If you are at college, university or in the armed forces, or for some other reason have no immediate access to a pastor, send us your book enclosing return postage and we will send it back to you with your certificate.

School of the Word
Harvestime Publishing Ltd
69 Main Street
Markfield
Leicester LE6 0UT
UK

Contents

Unless otherwise stated, Scripture quotations are taken from the New International Version.

Other versions referred to in this series include the New American Standard Bible (NASB), the Revised Authorised Version (RAV) and the Amplified Bible (Amp).

Verses have blank spaces for you to insert the missing words as you follow the Scriptures. This will deepen the impact of the Bible in your life.

School OF THE
WORD

Looking in the Mirror: Self-acceptance

1. Introduction

Men and women have *much in common*. Together they form part of the race of mankind which God created to exercise dominion over the rest of the created order. 'Male and female he created them. God blessed them and said to them, '. . . Subdue . . . rule . . .'' ' (Genesis 1:27-28).

In the plan of redemption men and women share equally in the benefits of Christ's cross. They are 'joint heirs of the grace of life' (1 Peter 3:7 RSV).

In other respects, however, men and women are *very different*. Their attitude to life, their emotional make-up, their means of fulfilment and their sexuality, for example, vary greatly.

In God's order, too, they have different roles to fulfil.

To develop our potential to the full, therefore, men must embrace their manhood and women their womanhood. The blurring of the difference, so common in our day, is a mark of departure from God's order.

This series of studies will point Christian men in the direction of being real men by the standard that really matters: God's revelation in Scripture.

2. Why Accept Yourself?

Until you learn to accept yourself you will never find your proper place in society and in the church. This includes accepting yourself as a man, and as the individual man that you are. *Why* should you do this?

a. Because Scripture assumes that you will

The Bible takes for granted that you will have a proper regard for yourself.

> *'Jesus replied: "Love the Lord your God with all your heart and with all your soul and with all your mind." This is the first and greatest commandment. And the second is like it: "Love your neighbour ____ _____ ."'*
>
> (Matthew 22:37-39)

This does not mean self-centred thinking or egotism but a healthy self-respect. See also Ephesians 5:28, 33.

b. Because it is God who made you and ordered your circumstances

To despise yourself is really to despise God who made you the person you are. To accept yourself is to accept that he has done a good job on you!

> *'I praise you because I am fearfully and wonderfully made; _____ _____ are wonderful, I know that full well.'*
>
> (Psalm 139:14)

This psalm is referring chiefly to a man's *physical body*. But God who 'in all things . . . works for the good of those who love him, who have been called according to his purpose' (Romans 8:28), also orders your *circumstances*.

Before his conversion Paul was a religious bigot and violent persecutor of believers in Jesus. After becoming a Christian, however, he accepted that God's hand had been upon him even in the circumstances of those preconversion days:

> *'I was advancing in Judaism beyond many Jews of my own age and was extremely zealous for the traditions of my fathers. But . . . God, who _____ ____ _____ _____ _____ and called me by his grace, was pleased to reveal his Son in me.'*
>
> (Galatians 1:14-16)

You may have had a difficult, painful or traumatic past. Now you need to accept that God was *for you* even in those trials, which *by faith* you can turn to your advantage.

c. Because, until you accept yourself, you cannot bless others

Some people are *proud*, with an inflated view of their own importance. Their pride cuts them off from other people. To such the Word of God is clear:

> 'Do not think of yourself _____ _____ _____ _____
> _____ , but rather think of yourself _____ _____
> _____ , in accordance with the measure of faith God
> has given you.'

> (Romans 12:3)

Many men, on the other hand, have the opposite problem; they have *a deficient view of their own worth*.

It is a spiritual principle that the view we have of ourselves is unconsciously projected out and shapes the view that others have of us. If you despise yourself, others will also despise you.

Saul, the first king of Israel, is a good illustration. Though blessed with a good family background (1 Samuel 9:1) and striking good looks (1 Samuel 9:2), plus an anointing for kingship (1 Samuel 10:1) and specially-conferred prophetic gifts (1 Samuel 10:9-11), he still *despised himself*. Consequently, when the time came for him to be presented to the people he ran off and hid among the baggage (1 Samuel 10:20-22).

He was eventually found and brought before the people. Some of them, however, reflecting his own self-image back upon him, '*despised him* and brought him no gifts' (1 Samuel 10:27). Unfortunately he never sought God's help with this problem. Though a head taller than the average man (1 Samuel 10:23), he remained small in his own eyes (1 Samuel 15:17) and so proved unable to succeed in his rule.

Until you, too, find a proper self-acceptance you will never be able to fulfil your true calling of being a unique blessing to others.

3. Areas of Common Dissatisfaction

Most men are unhappy about the features which, in the very nature of things, they cannot control or change:

a. Physical features

- 'My nose is too big' (or small, or pointed, or curved, or flat).

- 'I'm too short' (or tall, or skinny, or stout).

- 'My ears stick out too much.'

In the long run these factors are of little importance. Think of the great men of God described in Scripture. What information are we given about their physical features? Hardly any, because *their ministry didn't depend on such things*.

b. Background and parents

- 'My father was drunk most of the time.'

- 'My mother took so many tranquillisers that she seemed unaware of my existence.'

- 'I never received any encouragement to work hard at school, so I failed all my exams.'

By faith and determination these disadvantages can be turned round to your good. Think about the childhood experiences of Joseph (Genesis 37:2-11, 17-28) and David (1 Samuel 16:1-13). And what about Isaac's trauma (Genesis 22:9-13)? These men didn't let such things hinder their development as men of God.

c. Natural abilities

- 'If only I were more intelligent.'

- 'I'd love to be able to draw but I haven't an ounce of artistic ability in me.'

- 'If I were musical I could write new songs for the church.'

Paul gave good counsel to some Christians who wished they were financially better off so that they could give more. The same counsel can be applied to this matter of skills and abilities:

> 'If the _____ is there, the gift is acceptable
> according to what one _____ , not according to what he does
> _____ _____ .'

(2 Corinthians 8:12)

4. Signs of Self-rejection

Among many others we may note:

a. Inability to trust God

Because you feel he has done a poor job in making you the way you are, which is a major aspect of life, you cannot trust him for lesser things — a job, a wife, material needs, etc.

b. Perfectionism

Rewriting a letter a dozen times because you keep making minor mistakes is an example of this. It is good to have high standards and to keep improving but when the time and effort expended outweighs the value of the accomplishment it becomes self-rejection.

c. Over-attention to clothes

This can be an attempt to compensate for physical features you find unacceptable. Jesus said: 'Which of you by worrying can add one cubit to his *stature*? So why do you worry about *clothing*?' (Matthew 6:27-28 RAV).

d. Self-criticism

In the final analysis this is criticism of God who made you, which Scripture condemns:

> *'Woe to him who _____ with his _____ . . . .*
> *Does the _____ say to the _____ , "What are you*
> *making?" '*

> (Isaiah 45:9)

e. Lavish spending

You spend far more than you should — or can afford — to attract the admiration you feel you do not merit for what you are.

f. Ungodly priorities

Giving yourself to a sport or artistic enterprise which you have proved to be good at, for example, can point to self-rejection if it draws you away from your walk with the Lord. (See Matthew 6:33.)

5. Satan's Lies About You

a. 'God has cheated you of your rights'

You have immense potential for God and his kingdom. Satan knows this and wants to prevent its development, so he tells you that God has given you a raw deal and cheated you of your rights to good looks, a nice family background, certain skills, etc.

This is the very ploy that he used with Eve in Eden. Eve knew God's command regarding the forbidden fruit and the penalty for eating it, but she listened to Satan instead.

16

> " 'You will not surely die," the serpent said to the woman. "For God knows that when you eat of it your _____ _____ ____ _____ , and you will be _____ _____ , knowing good and evil." '
>
> (Genesis 3:4-5)

He implied that God was withholding from her something that it was her right to have. She believed the lie and fell. If you believe the same lie, you rob yourself of the blessing of God on your future. You will only be half a man.

b. 'Compare yourself with Fred and see what a failure you are'

Satan gets the extrovert who is free in praise and worship to compare himself with the introvert who is studious and good at opening up the Word. And vice versa. The extrovert concludes: 'I'm all froth and bubble with no substance; I'm a failure!' The introvert concludes: 'I'm all bookish and bound up instead of being outgoing like him; I'm a failure!'

Such comparison always begets despair — so don't do it!

> 'When they _____ themselves by themselves and _____ themselves with themselves, they are _____ _____ .'
>
> (2 Corinthians 10:12)

Some qualities can and should be imitated: faith, love, patience, courage, etc. Timothy was urged to 'set an example for the believers in speech, in life, in love, in faith and in purity' (1 Timothy 4:12). These are *character qualities*.

> 'Remember your leaders . . . . Consider the outcome of their way of life and _____ _____ _____ .'
>
> (Hebrews 13:7)

Others are *personality traits* and *personal circumstances*. These should *not* be imitated: being quick-witted or studious; having certain mannerisms or accent; appearance; natural skills; etc.

6. The Truth About Yourself

Knowing the truth about yourself will set you free to be the man God wants you to be (John 8:32).

a. God planned you before birth

This included the 'defects' you would like to change but can't.

> *'My frame was not hidden from you when I was _____ in the _____ _____ . When I was woven together in the depths of the earth, your eyes saw my _____ _____ . All the days ordained for me were written in your book _____ _____ ___ _____ _____ ___ ___ .'*

(Psalm 139:15-16)

b. God is still working on you

Though you are accepted by God in Jesus Christ, the process of becoming more completely what you are still goes on. Like an unfinished picture, you are not yet complete. So don't write yourself off too soon!

> *'We _____ God's workmanship.'*

(Ephesians 2:10)

That word 'are' is a present continuous tense. The Master Craftsman is still working on you. Be sure to co-operate with him (see the 'co-operator's prayer' in Psalm 138:8).

c. Outward and temporal ideals don't matter

Outward appearance, the 'right' family background and particular skills have little relevance to spiritual and eternal things. The fact that Jesus' appearance is not even mentioned (except the disfigurement caused by his sufferings — Isaiah 52:14; 53:2-3), that he was born in a stable and that he never attended the rabbinical schools, did not stop God using him. The same holds true for Christian men today.

> *'Do not consider his _____ or his _____ ,*
> *for I have rejected him. The Lord does not look at the things man*
> *looks at. Man looks at the _____ appearance, but the*
> *Lord looks at the _____ .'*

(1 Samuel 16:7)

d. Becoming like Jesus is all-important

Here is a *character* goal — one we all have an equal opportunity of achieving! Your true happiness and fulfilment lies in becoming like the man Christ Jesus. Developing the character of Christ as described in Galatians 5:22-23 is worth far more than having a hair transplant or polishing up your accent.

> *'Those God foreknew he also predestined to be conformed to*
> _____ _____ ____ _____ *Son.'*

(Romans 8:29)

This is what Paul longed for in his converts, 'for whom', he said, 'I am again in the pains of childbirth *until Christ is formed in you*' (Galatians 4:19). True manhood is a *character* business!

7. What to Do Now

a. Give the externals due attention

If your hairstyle is weird, change it. If you have sweaty feet, wash them and change your socks more often. If you failed in school, consider evening classes.

In other words, take sensible steps to ensure that none of these negative factors hinders your usefulness in the Lord's service. You could ask a trusted friend or pastor for advice here.

b. Accept what you cannot change

Unless the Lord sees fit to change things supernaturally, accept your remaining 'defects'. In fact, you can turn them for good. How? By seeing them as *a stimulus to rely more on the Lord*.

If you have a facial scar or birthmark, for instance, people will not flock to you for your good looks. So it must be the character of Jesus in you that attracts them. Develop character and learn to live unselfconsciously with the 'defect'. This was Paul's attitude to his 'thorn in the flesh':

> *'I pleaded with the Lord to take it away from me. But he said to me, "My _____ is sufficient for you, for my power is made perfect in _____ . "Therefore I will boast all the more gladly about my _____ , so that Christ's _____ may rest on me.'*
>
> (2 Corinthians 12:8-9)

c. Picture yourself as a man of God

God made you. God saved you. God loves you and has his hand on you. He has a destiny for you to fulfil. So learn to see yourself that way – a blessing on two legs taking the presence of Christ wherever you go (2 Corinthians 2:14).

Put a 'Man of God' sticker on your mirror and smile at the grace of God reflected back to you when you look at yourself. Learn to say with Paul:

> *'By the _____ of God I am what I am, and his grace to me was not _____ _____ .'*
>
> (1 Corinthians 15:10)

True Christian manhood begins here, in accepting yourself as a man of immense worth and limitless potential. Embark on the adventure now!

****

LESSON 1

Looking in the Mirror: Self-acceptance

True or False

1.   T F   For a man to reject himself — his appearance, his background and his natural skills (or lack of them) — is really to reject God, who made him.

2.   T F   It is possible to despise yourself and still be a blessing to others.

3.   T F   The things about ourselves that we would most like to change are usually the things we are unable to change.

4.   T F   Lack of ability to trust God for a job, a wife or money to pay a mortgage could be a sign of self-rejection.

5.   T F   Satan tells us that God has done a good job with us.

6.   T F   Character qualities such as faith and patience can and should be imitated, but personality traits should not.

7.   T F   God finished working on us the moment we were born again.

8.   T F   Real manhood means becoming increasingly like the greatest man of all — Jesus.

9.   T F   God made me. He loves me right now. He accepts me and has a purpose for my life.

Group Discussion

1.   Encourage each other by going round the group telling each man the features of his life and character which are a blessing to you.

2. 'The grass is always greener on the other side of the fence.' How does this saying highlight the foolishness of wrong comparisons? Give personal examples of how you have fallen for this lie of the enemy.

3. A man lacking in love and concern for others is a man with a self-acceptance problem. Explain this in the light of Matthew 22:39.

Personal Assignment

1. Begin to compile a list of Scriptures which emphasise your value and potential as a man in God's eyes. Write them out and review them. You could start with Galatians 2:20b: 'The Son of God . . . loved *me* and gave himself for *me*.'

2. Tell the Lord you are sorry for your rejection of his design for you. Then thank him for the way he has ordered your life so far and tell him that from now on you intend to co-operate with him in becoming a real man.

True or False

1.T 2.F 3.T 4.T 5.F 6.T 7.F 8.T 9.T

School OF THE WORD

The Real Man: Character-formation

We have begun to see in lesson 1 that true manhood has little to do with rippling muscles, craggy features or being good at football. Being a real man lies in being like Jesus, and that is to do with *character*.

Now we need to look more closely at this area. We all know that muscles can be developed by exercise, but how do you develop character? What exactly *is* character anyway?

1. What is Character?

The dictionary defines character as 'moral strength' or 'moral quality'. It is the essential you. It is what you are *when you are alone*, and it contrasts with *personality*, which is the expression of yourself to others.

Ideally, the two should coincide, your personality expressing your character.

Character qualities can be *acquired* and *developed*. They include the ones listed by Peter:

> 'Make _____ _____ to add to your **faith goodness**; and to goodness, **knowledge**; and to knowledge, **self-control**; and to self-control, **perseverance**; and to perseverance, **godliness**; and to godliness, **brotherly kindness**; and to brotherly kindness. **love**. For if you possess these qualities ____ _____ _____ , they will keep you from being ineffective and unproductive in your knowledge of our Lord Jesus Christ.'
>
> (2 Peter 1:5-8)

When a man becomes a Christian, the Holy Spirit begins to stimulate the growth of such qualities. Paul refers to them in Galatians 5:22-23 as 'the *fruit of the Spirit*': love, joy, peace, patience, kindness, goodness, faithfulness, gentleness and self-control.

Yet another list of character qualities is found in the *beatitudes* of Matthew 5:3-12. Jesus, the perfect man, exemplified them all.

2. The Elements of Character

The present state of your character is the result of several different influences.

a. Built-in moral standards and conscience

Because human beings are made in God's image (Genesis 1:26-27), they have a built-in sense of right and wrong. Though tarnished by the Fall (Genesis 3), the image is not destroyed completely.

> 'The wrath of God is being revealed from heaven against all the godlessness and wickedness of men who suppress the truth by their wickedness, since what may be _____ _____ _____ is _____ ____ _____ , because God has made it plain to them. For since the creation of the world God's invisible qualities — his eternal power and divine nature — have been clearly seen, being understood from what has been made, so that men are _____ _____ .'
>
> (Romans 1:18-20)

b. Childhood training and experience

This will include a variety of factors, including:

1. Birth order

First-born children, for instance, tend to be fairly aggressive, mature and able to respond to authority, while secondborns are generally more easygoing, loyal and soft-hearted. This whole area is well documented in Barbara Sullivan's *Your Place in the Family* (Marshall Pickering) [in the USA, *Firstborn, Secondborn* (Chosen Books)].

2. Love, discipline, instruction and example

The way your parents treated you has helped form your present character. Perhaps their *example* is the most powerful factor.

Eli is a good illustration. Though a priest of Israel, he was greedy and self-indulgent (1 Samuel 2:29), and so grew very fat (1 Samuel 4:18). It is not surprising that his sons, who also were priests, followed his example (1 Samuel 2:12-17), their self-indulgence extending to sexual matters. Little wonder Eli's rebuke was so weak (1 Samuel 2:22-25) — he was hardly an example of self-discipline!

If you had a bad background, don't worry. This need not hold you back from godly character! *God* is your Father now; you have inherited his nature (see 2 Peter 1:4; 1 John 3:9) and his is the example to follow:

> 'Be _____ *of God, therefore, as dearly loved*
> _____ .'

(Ephesians 5:1)

3. Temperament

This is the combination of inner characteristics you inherited from your parents. You may be an introvert or an extrovert. You may be the back-slapping type, the life and soul of the party, company-loving and talkative. Or maybe you're a natural loner, thoughtful and creative.

There are infinite variations, each with both good and bad aspects. You will find the subject treated in detail in Tim LaHaye's *Spirit Controlled Temperament*.

3. Getting to Grips with Changing

Character can be changed! The development of true manhood consists in becoming more and more like Jesus. There is no such thing, of course, as *instant* Christlikeness. It is a lifelong process, and the best time to start is now!

> 'We, who with unveiled faces all reflect the Lord's glory, _____
> _____ _____ into his _____
> with ever-increasing glory.'
>
> (2 Corinthians 3:18)

The word *transformed* here is from the Greek *metamorphosis*. In biology, metamorphosis is the process by which a caterpillar, for example, becomes a butterfly — a total change, from the inside out. Be encouraged to believe that by being 'metamorphosed' into the likeness of Jesus, real manhood is within your grasp, whatever your present situation.

How, then, do we go about it?

4. Clear the Past

a. Forget it!

When you became a Christian the 'old you' came to an end. It was buried in your baptism and should be left there! A 'new you' came into being, with all the potential for true manhood, free from the shackles of the past:

> 'If anyone is in Christ, he is a _____ _____ ; the old
> has _____ , the _____ has come!'
>
> (2 Corinthians 5:17)

Forget childhood weaknesses and accusations of being 'soft' or 'tied to mother's apron strings'. Forget the bullying you may have done to others, or the smoking and under-age drinking that was supposed to make you more manly. Forget them because God has forgotten them:

> 'Their sins and lawless acts I will _____ _____
> _____ .'
>
> (Hebrews 10:17)

To *forget* in this context does not mean to erase from the memory. That is impossible. It means to *refuse to dwell on those issues any more*, for they have been dealt with at the cross. Don't let Satan tie you down to those past weaknesses again. Instead, affirm:

> *'Forgetting what is behind and straining towards what is _____ , I press on towards _____ _____ .'*
>
> (Philippians 3:13-14)

The goal for you right now is true Christian manhood based on the character of Christ.

> *'When I was a child, I talked like a child, I thought like a child, I _____ like a child. When I became a man, I put _____ _____ _____ ____ .'*
>
> (1 Corinthians 13:11)

b. Believe that 'iniquity' is dealt with

Of the many Bible words for sin, the word *iniquity* has a particular link with heredity. It points to sin springing from weaknesses that run in the family:

> 'I, the Lord your God, am a jealous God, visiting the **iniquity** of the fathers on the children to the third and fourth generations of those who hate me, but showing mercy to thousands, to those who love me and keep my commandments.'
>
> (Exodus 20:5-6 RAV)

As a believer, you come in the latter category, not the former! Is there behind you a family line of weak-willed men, of brutal tyrants, of sexual deviants? With *you*, being in Christ, a new family line of true men of God can begin, because:

> *'We all, like sheep, have gone astray, each of us has turned to his own way; and the Lord has laid on him [Jesus] the _____ of us all.'*
>
> (Isaiah 53:6)

Claim your deliverance and break free for better things!

5. Start Thinking God's Way

Become single-minded for God. Anchor your thought-life firmly into him. 'Seek first his kingdom and his righteousness' (Matthew 6:33). That's how to become a man.

> *'Do not conform any longer to the pattern of this world, but be _____ by the _____ of your _____ .'*
>
> (Romans 12:2)

There's that word *transformed* again — metamorphosis! And Paul tells us how it can be your experience: 'by the renewing of your mind'.

Take your thought life in hand. Exercise manly control over it. Determine to reject soap-opera morality and tee-shirt slogans such as: 'If it feels good, do it.' Instead, soak your mind in the life-giving truth of Scripture. Read it and memorise it until Christlike thinking and living become second nature:

> *'We demolish arguments and every pretension that sets itself up against the knowledge of God, and we take captive every _____ to make it _____ ____ _____ .'*
>
> (2 Corinthians 10:5)

A man of the Book is a man of God, and a man of God is a man indeed.

6. Sanctify Your Imagination

We all have a cinema screen in our heads. Films, in which we ourselves are the leading actors, are shown continually on that screen of the imagination.

How you see yourself in those films is constantly shaping your character. What you see is what you are *becoming*. So it is vital to let the Lord into this area of your thinking. (See Proverbs 23:7a NASB.)

When the twelve spies went to view the promised land, they met giants there. On their return, the majority reported:

> 'We can't attack those people; they are stronger than we are
> . . . . We seemed like grasshoppers ____ _____ _____
> _____ , and we looked the same ____ _____ .'

(Numbers 13:31, 33)

Even as they spoke, they were viewing an imagination-film in which they were overshadowed by these giants, cringing before them and suffering crushing defeat. No wonder they never entered the promised land but died in the wilderness!

Joshua and Caleb, by contrast, let the *promises of God* dictate both their faith and the mental films they watched. God had promised to *give* them the land (Numbers 13:2). So even though they had seen the same giants as the other spies, they reported:

> 'We should go up and take possession of the land, for we can
> _____ ____ ____ .'

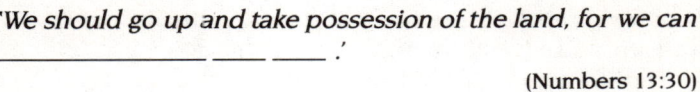

(Numbers 13:30)

On the screen of their imagination they were slaying giants by the dozen on the strength of God's promise! In due course the 'film' became reality. They entered the land in victory.

Become a film-producer and imagine yourself as the man of God portrayed in the promises of Scripture. That is what you will become!

7. Confess Your Faith as a Man

Don't reinforce the old weaknesses by confessing them:

— 'I'm lazy and undisciplined.'

— 'When it comes to decision-making, I'm hopeless.'

— 'I can't stand people.'

— 'The responsibility of being a husband gets me down.'

Don't tell lies, either:

— 'I've got a will of iron!'

— 'There's no-one more decisive than me.'

— 'I'm the life and soul of the party.'

— 'I deserve the Husband of the Year award.'

Your confession must *match your level of belief* about yourself. What you believe is what you confess. This principle is well illustrated by Paul in the context of salvation:

> 'If you **confess** with your mouth, "Jesus is Lord," and **believe** in your heart that God raised him from the dead, you will be saved. For it is with your _____ that you _____ and are justified, and it is with your _____ that you _____ and are saved.'

(Romans 10:9-10)

Do you believe that the Lord is steadily changing you as you seek to become a true man of God? Then let your confession match your faith:

— 'I'm a lot more disciplined than I was.'

— 'The Lord's really helping me become more decisive.'

— 'Sociability is an art I'm slowly learning.'

— 'I'm gradually getting a grip on the responsibility of being a husband.'

8. Actively Obey the Lord

This is the most important step of all, and one that you must take a dozen times a day.

At a wedding in Cana, obedience to Jesus resulted in a miracle — water became wine:

> *'His mother said to the servants, "____ _____ ____*
> *_____ _____ ." '*

(John 2:5)

Miracles still happen through doing whatever he says. Weak men become strong; hard-bitten men become gentle and considerate; effeminate men become truly masculine; men like Adam become men like Christ!

How can we know what the Lord wants us to do?

a. Through the Scriptures

Suppose you tend to be a man-pleaser. You see from the Gospels how Jesus confronted the hypocrisy of the Pharisees. Confrontation has not been your strong point so far but now you determine that when necessary you will do it. Then do it!

b. By the indwelling Holy Spirit

It is his function to make Jesus known. Jesus himself said:

> *'The Spirit will take from what is _____ and make it known*
> *____ _____ .'*

(John 16:15)

Be sensitive, therefore, to the Spirit's promptings in your heart. If he says: 'Go and tell Bill it's a pleasure to work with him,' do it!

c. Through mature Christians, especially leaders

Learn to hear God through others. If a caring elder tells you that you need to be swayed more by truth and less by sentiment, take it seriously.

****

LESSON 2

The Real Man:
Character-formation

True or False

1. T F The qualities described in Galatians 5:22-23 and 2 Peter 1:5-8 are character qualities.

2. T F All men know the basic difference between right and wrong.

3. T F It is possible for character to be changed.

4. T F It is healthy to dwell on the sins and weaknesses of our preconversion days.

5. T F Jesus is the example of perfect manhood.

6. T F Hereditary weaknesses will unfortunately always be with us.

7. T F Bible meditation and memorisation is the best way to renew the mind.

8. T F Our imagination shapes our future.

9. T F Feelings are more important than deliberate obedience to the Word of God.

Group Discussion

1. Encourage each other with testimonies of how you have changed already. Be specific, giving concrete examples of the kind of situation where the change is apparent.

2. What is the world's view of manliness as portrayed in the media? How far does the character of Jesus as shown in the Gospels match that view?

3. Why is it so hard to change? What can we do to help one another when we feel like giving up?

Personal Assignment

1. Make an honest attempt to list both your character strengths and your character weaknesses. Then give the list to your wife or a close, trusted friend and ask them to add to it or adjust it. Insist that you want the truth, the whole truth and nothing but the truth!

2. Pinpoint the most obvious area of weakness and plan how, with God's help, you will tackle it. Search out appropriate Scripture verses, copy them and memorise them. Then start changing!

True or False

1.T 2.T 3.T 4.F 5.T 6.F 7.T 8.T 9.F

School OF THE
WORD

Temple Maintenance: Controlling the body

One part of the Spirit's character-fruit is, as we have seen, self-control. And what more natural way to exercise it than in the manly mastery of our *bodies*!

'You were bought at a price,' Paul reminds us. 'Therefore *honour God with your body*' (1 Corinthians 6:20). In fact, we are urged to offer our bodies 'as living sacrifices, holy and pleasing to God' (Romans 12:1), and so to exalt Christ by means of them (Philippians 1:20).

Manhood from a bodily point of view, then, is not so much to have a 'Mr Universe' physique as to 'offer yourselves to God . . . and offer the parts of your body to him as instruments of righteousness' (Romans 6:13).

1. The Body is Important

Some teach that the body is a hindrance, tying us down to this material world, and that what matters is the realm of the spirit, where we can soar away to higher things. But this is not biblical Christianity; it is more the emphasis of eastern religion and unscriptural philosophy. The body is important:

a. Because Jesus came in bodily form

He didn't come purely as a spirit-being.

> 'When Christ came into the world, he said, "Sacrifice and offering you did not desire, but __ _____ you prepared for me." '
>
> (Hebrews 10:5)

John expresses it another way. 'The Word,' he says, '*became flesh*' (John 1:14).

b. Because Jesus has a glorified body *now*

After his resurrection Jesus did not 'graduate' out of his body to some higher spirit-realm. He retained a real body. On one occasion, having risen from the dead, he said to his disciples, who thought they were seeing a ghost:

> '*Look at my _____ and my _____ . It is I myself! Touch me and see; a ghost does not have _____ and _____ , as you see I have.*'
>
> (Luke 24:39)

His resurrection body did, however, have *greater powers*. He apparently had the ability, for example, to appear in a locked room without coming through the door (John 20:19-20, 26).

In this same resurrection body he later ascended to the Father's presence (Acts 1:9-10). He has that same body now.

c. Because our bodies are called 'temples of the Holy Spirit'

A temple is the very special and highly honoured place where a god dwells.

> '*Do you not know that _____ _____ is a temple of the _____ _____ , who is in you, whom you have received from God?*'
>
> (1 Corinthians 6:19)   .

Our bodies are worthy of great honour if the Holy Spirit of God has chosen to live there.

d. Because Scripture assumes that we care for our bodies

To give attention to your body is not a waste of time. It is natural and proper.

> *'Husbands ought to love their wives ____ _____ _____*
> *_____ . He who loves his wife loves himself. After all, no-*
> *one ever _____ his own body, but he _____ and*
> *_____ _____ ___ .'*

(Ephesians 5:28-29)

e. Jesus' healing ministry confirmed the body's value

A large proportion of the public ministry of Jesus was devoted to restoring sick and ailing bodies to healthy normality. His was not merely a ministry of 'saving souls'. He addressed the needs of the whole person, the body included.

f. Our eternal state is to be a bodily one

Our ultimate destiny, after Christ ushers in the eternal state at his return, is to have a *resurrection body like his*. We shall not for ever be spirit-beings. The transformation that will take place is called by Paul 'the redemption of our bodies' (Romans 8:23). Elsewhere he describes it as being 'clothed with our heavenly dwelling', in contrast to 'this tent', or mortal body, in which we now live (2 Corinthians 5:4).

> *'Our citizenship is in heaven. And we eagerly await a Saviour*
> *from there, the Lord Jesus Christ, who, by the power that enables*
> *him to bring everything under his control, will transform our*
> *_____ _____ so that they will be like _____*
> *_____ _____ .'*

(Philippians 3:20-21)

2. The Body has Certain Needs and Drives

The body's needs and drives are all God-given and therefore good.

37

a. Hunger and thirst

A healthy appetite and good food to satisfy it is one of God's great ideas:

> 'He satisfies the _____ and fills the _____ with
> _____ _____ .'

(Psalm 107:9)

b. The sex drive

Sex was God's gift *before* the Fall:

> '*Male and female he created them. God _____ them
> and said to them, "Be _____ and increase in number;
> fill the earth." '*

(Genesis 1:27-28)

The sex drive was given not only for *procreation* but for *pleasure* in the sealing of the love and commitment between a man and his wife. See Proverbs 5:18-19 (where 'fountain' means the body parts that produce life).

c. Sleep

Sleep is the divinely-appointed means by which we recover from the exertion of daily living:

> '*I will lie down and sleep ____ _____ , for you alone, O
> Lord, make me dwell in safety.'*

(Psalm 4:8)

d. Exercise

Movement and action are the natural outworking of a healthy body, especially when the blessing of God puts a spring in the step:

> '*For you who revere my name, the sun of righteousness will rise
> with healing in its wings. And you will go out and _____ like
> _____ _____ _____ _____ _____ .'*

(Malachi 4:2)

38

3. Manly Self-Control

While it is true that all these physical drives are God-given and good, they can quickly get out of hand if not kept in check. They then become means by which sin can take hold.

The best preventive against bodily excess is the development of the *spiritual* side of your being:

> *'Live by the _____ , and you will not gratify the desires of the flesh.'*
>
> (Galatians 5:16 margin)

Only when the impulses of the body and soul (mind, will and emotions) are kept subservient to your spiritual drive will you enjoy true freedom in living. Paul saw the importance of manly self-control in this area when he said:

> *'I _____ my body and make it my _____ so that after I have preached to others, I myself will not be disqualified for the prize.'*
>
> (1 Corinthians 9:27)

How, in practice, can we exercise this self-control? What does it mean in real terms to 'beat' our bodies and make them our slaves? It will include:

a. Right eating and drinking, and fasting

1. Balanced diet

A balanced diet is necessary for good health. There is a considerable amount of literature available on the subject which can point us in the right direction without making us food faddists.

2. Moderation

We should eat and drink in moderate quantities, in keeping with our workload and metabolism:

'Listen, my son, and be wise, and keep your heart on the right path. Do not join those who drink _____ _____ wine or _____ themselves on meat, for _____ and _____ become poor, and drowsiness clothes them in rags.'

(Proverbs 23:19-21)

3. Drinking

A biblical life-style permits wine-drinking, but forbids excess:

'Do not get _____ on wine, which leads to debauchery. Instead, be filled with the _____ .'

(Ephesians 5:18)

This verse points clearly to being filled with the Holy Spirit as a key to avoiding bodily excess. A man filled with the Spirit, part of whose fruit is self-control, will be able to exercise proper moderation.

4. Fussiness

A real man will not be over-fussy about his food. A long list of dislikes is a social handicap and a childish trait. Far better to develop an adventurous approach to food and drink:

'If some unbeliever invites you to a meal and you want to go, _____ whatever is put _____ _____ without raising _____ of conscience.'

(1 Corinthians 10:27)

While the context of this verse is one of food previously offered to pagan gods, the principle of not upsetting your host holds good: even if you don't like cabbage, eat it up 'like a man'! See also Luke 10:5-8.

5. Fasting

Fasting is an excellent way of showing your body who's boss.

Always fast with a *specific purpose*. If you decide to miss lunch once a week, for example, be sure to spend the lunch break in purposeful prayer, Bible meditation or Scripture memorisation.

The Bible *assumes* that we will fast from time to time. Jesus, who said: 'When [not if] you *pray*' (Matthew 6:6) also said: 'When [not if] you *fast*' (Matthew 6:16). See also Acts 13:2-3.

b. Sexual restraints

The only permissible avenue of sexual expression is *within the marriage bond*:

> *'Since there is so much* _____ *, each man should have his own* _____ *, and each woman her own* _____ *.'*

(1 Corinthians 7:2)

Today, the world sees it as manly to be sexually promiscuous. It views sexual purity as the opposite of macho virility. This is a sad distortion of the truth! It is to Timothy as a 'man of God' — a real man — that Paul addresses the exhortation: 'keep yourself *pure*' (1 Timothy 5:22).

> *'It is better to* _____ *than to* _____ _____ _____ *.'*

(1 Corinthians 7:9)

This verse points to marriage as the only legitimate outlet for the strong male sex drive. The implication is that other outlets are *not* legitimate, including:

-   *perversion*: homosexual acts, transexuality, transvestism, etc.

-   *self-gratification*: masturbation, pornography, etc.

There is great power in purity! Make a covenant with your eyes (Job 31:1) and avoid temptation.

c. An ordered life

Sleep is a gift of God, and rest and relaxation are necessary if we are to function efficiently. But unless we take care, we can quickly lapse into idleness and time-wasting.

Discover your sleep requirements and, as far as possible, tailor the rest of your life accordingly. If you need seven hours of sleep, don't take nine. For most men, the set hours of their employment give a basic structure to their working day. If, out of every twenty-four hours, you sleep eight and work eight, that still leaves you eight to organise — more than enough time to do all you want to do and ought to do.

Plan those precious eight hours in order to use them to the best advantage:

> 'Be careful how you walk, not as unwise men, but as wise, **making the most of your time**, because the days are evil.'
> (Ephesians 5:15-16 NASB)

Set goals in every area of life. Check periodically as to how well you are succeeding. Don't let the TV rule your life. Be a man and exert your mastery over time and leisure!

d. Fitness and grooming

Until the twentieth century the normal demands of everyday living provided most people with adequate physical exercise. Many walked miles to work and used a variety of muscles doing jobs which today require little more effort than the pressing of a button. We ride in cushioned comfort from one place to another and, in between, let machines do most of our work.

Mind, emotions and spirit function best in a healthy body. Since normal living today often fails to keep us physically fit, as responsible men we deliberately need to build some kind of exercise into our personal schedule.

> 'Physical _____ is of _____ _____ , but *godliness has value for all things, holding promise for both the present life and the life to come.'*
> (1 Timothy 4:8)

If physical exercise was of 'some value' in Paul's era, how much more so today! While manliness is not to be measured in terms of physique, ball skills or sporting prowess, every man who takes the gift of his body seriously will organise himself *some* regular exercise.

It goes without saying that *smoking* and *drug-taking* have absolutely no place in the life of a man of God. They offer no benefits whatever and are proven dangers to good health. We dare not pollute the temple of the Holy Spirit with such activities.

Proper attention to personal hygiene and good grooming will add the finishing touches of proper self-respect to a man of God healthy in spirit, soul and body:

> 'May God himself, the God of peace, sanctify you through and
> through. May your whole _____ , _____ and _____
> be kept blameless at the coming of our Lord Jesus Christ.'
>
> (1 Thessalonians 5:23)

e. Appearance and mannerisms

These should express our *male identity*. The blurring of the difference between the sexes so common in our generation is strongly opposed by the teaching of Scripture:

> 'A woman must not wear men's clothing, nor a _____ wear
> _____ _____ , for the Lord your God
> _____ anyone who does this.'
>
> (Deuteronomy 22:5)

This is not to deny a woman her slacks or a Scotsman his kilt but to warn against the onset of transvestism or similar sexual perversion. In general, avoid clothing which is likely to be considered effeminate. The same applies to hair:

> 'Does not the very nature of things teach you that if a man has
> _____ _____ , it is a _____ to him?'
>
> (1 Corinthians 11:14)

The expression 'the very nature of things' here probably refers (as in Romans 1:26; 2:14, 27) to *God's* design for nature rather than just traditional attitudes or cultural considerations. It seems that God requires one clear mark of masculine identity to be the *shortness of a man's hair* in comparison to a woman's.

Obviously, length is a relative affair. A crew cut is not necessarily the ultimate in godliness! But long hair is meant to be a distinctively female characteristic and is not compatible with true masculinity.

Ensure that your mannerisms, style of walking and tone of voice are manly rather than effeminate. Trusted friends or leaders will set you on the right lines.

* *

LESSON 3

Temple Maintenance:
Controlling the body

True or False

1. T F Paul teaches us in 1 Corinthians 6:20 that we are to honour God with our spirits.

2. T F Eastern religion plays down the value of the body but biblical Christianity sees the body as of great importance.

3. T F After his resurrection and ascension, Jesus graduated from his body to a higher spiritual realm.

4. T F To call our bodies, as Paul does, temples of the Holy Spirit, is to accord them high honour.

5. T F The body's need for food and drink, sex, sleep and exercise is God-given and good.

6. T F We can indulge our bodily appetites to the full because they were given to us by God.

7. T F Fasting is a valuable exercise in bodily self-control.

8.   T F One expression of our manliness can be the mastery of our time by an ordered life.

9.   T F God wants women to look like women and men to look like women.

Group Discussion

1.   Share how God has already altered your thinking on some of the topics covered in this lesson.

2.   Discuss the bodily image of manhood put across in advertisements, films, books and TV. Are *any* of these features compatible with the approach to manhood presented in this lesson?

3.   In what ways can an unhealthy body, prone to sickness, affect your spiritual life, emotional life and spiritual life? Give real examples from your own experience.

Personal Assignment

1.   List the practical changes you need to make in eating habits, sexual practices, time-planning, etc. in order to make your body a better vehicle through which Christ can express himself to the world.

2.   Do a careful study of Romans chapter 6. Note and begin to put into practice the lessons you learn from it regarding the use of your body.

True or False

1. F 2.T 3. F 4.T 5.T 6.F 7.T 8.T 9. F

Feelings without Shame: Emotional Freedom

1. Introduction

'Men have minds; women have emotions' is an over-generalisation, to say the least! It is true, however, that emotions are less active in men than in women *of the same temperament*.

Refusal to accept emotions has produced the 'stiff upper lip' mentality: even if your wife and children have just died, your job has been lost and your house is falling down, you just keep a cool demeanour and carry on as if nothing has happened! Men *do* have emotions, however, and should accept them.

Acceptance does not mean bursting into tears every five minutes. It means finding a stable balance between emotional expression and emotional control, combining sensitivity with firmness so as to be, like Abraham Lincoln, 'a man of steel and velvet'. This balance is one that most women greatly appreciate in a man.

2. Where Do Emotions Come From?

A proper appreciation of the source of your emotions will help you face them rightly.

a. The image of God in man

Emotion has its origin in the nature of God himself. When he 'created man in his own image' (Genesis 1:27) God built into man the emotional dimension of his own being.

Not surprisingly, Scripture attributes many emotions to God, including:

- *Wrath (or anger)* This is a fierce hatred of evil, steady and continuous, not expressed in fits of irrational pique:

  > 'God is a righteous judge, a God who _____
  > _____ _____ every day.'
  >
  > (Psalm 7:11)

See also Hebrews 3:7-11.

- *Love* This love is no passing fancy; it is active and consistent: 'God is love' (1 John 4:16).

- *Compassion* An ability to appreciate the sorrows through which his people are passing:

  > 'The Lord is gracious and _____ , slow to
  > anger and rich in _____ . The Lord is good to all; he has
  > _____ on all he has made.'
  >
  > (Psalm 145:8-9)

b. The example of Jesus

The nature of God the Father was perfectly expressed in Jesus, the ideal man. No-one has ever seen God, but Jesus has 'made him known' (John 1:18). 'I always do what pleases him,' he claimed (John 8:29) — and this included his emotional expression. Notice:

- *Sorrow* Jesus did not hold with the notion that real men never cry. At the tomb of Lazarus, 'Jesus wept' (John 11:35). He shed tears, too, over the city of Jerusalem as he foresaw the horrors of its destruction (Luke 19:41-44).

- *Anger* The child's prayer: 'Gentle Jesus, meek and mild,' expresses only one side of Jesus' character. True, he could take little ones on his knee and bless them, but he could also be forceful in his righteous anger. Imagine his flashing eyes and passionate tones as he denounced the self-righteous:

> 'Woe to you, teachers of the law and Pharisees, you _____ !
> You are like _____ _____ , which look
> beautiful on the outside but on the inside are full of dead men's
> bones and everything unclean.'
>
> (Matthew 23:27)

In the synagogue where the man with a shrivelled hand awaited healing, Jesus met opposition from some who viewed healing as work and therefore forbidden on the Sabbath. His emotions were stirred by their attitude:

> 'He looked round at them _____ _____ and, _____
> _____ at their stubborn hearts, said to the man,
> "Stretch out your hand." He stretched it out, and his hand was
> completely restored.'
>
> (Mark 3:5)

See also Jesus' anger at the cleansing of the temple (John 2:13-17).

— *Love* The New Testament is full of the love of Jesus, ranging from his affection for individuals to his self-sacrificial love for the church (see John 11:5; 13:1; Ephesians 5:25).

— *Compassion*

> 'When Jesus landed and saw a large crowd, he had compassion
> on them, because they were like _____ _____
> __ _____ .'
>
> (Mark 6:34)

c. The effects of sin

We have seen that the image of God in man is the source of our emotions. The Fall, however, tarnished that image, spoiling every part of our being. That is why there is so much emotional imbalance and misdirection in men today.

In Christ things are put right. Once we are born again and filled with the Holy Spirit, our emotions can find healing through the process of sanctification. Are you over-emotional? Or, more likely, under-emotional?

Study the life of Jesus and ask the Holy Spirit to bring your emotional life into line with his.

3. Factors Governing Our Emotions

a. Physiological

Glandular malfunctions and other physical deficiencies can have an adverse effect on our emotions. All the more reason for maintaining a healthy body! But even healthy men vary greatly in the degree of emotion they are prone to feel. God has made us all different.

b. Psychological

Knowing that on Friday you finish work to go on holiday can give an emotional lift. So can falling in love! Conversely, the end of a period of mental or emotional concentration can produce depression. Just as hard physical work leads to *physical* tiredness, intense concentration (such as putting on a play or taking part in some 'big day') leads to the *emotional* tiredness of anticlimax.

c. Behavioural

How we behave governs our feelings. Cain gives us a good example:

> *'The Lord looked with favour on Abel and his offering, but on Cain and his offering he did not look with favour. So Cain was very _____ , and his face was _____ . Then the Lord said to Cain, "Why are you angry? Why is your face downcast? If you _____ ___ _____ , will you not be accepted?" '*

(Genesis 4:4-7)

More literally, that last sentence could be translated: 'If you do well, *will not your countenance* [face] *be lifted up?*' (NASB) or: 'If you had done the right thing, *you would be smiling*' (Good News Bible).

Bad behaviour (sin) produces bad feelings, which are expressed in frowns and angry looks. Right behaviour, on the other hand, produces good feelings, expressed in smiles. Are you living righteously? (We will take up this point again later.)

4. The Dangers of Uncontrolled Emotion

a. A roller-coaster existence

By their very nature, feelings are largely unpredictable. They come and go, high and low. If we allow our actions to be governed by our feelings, therefore, we shall have a life of instability, double-mindedness and indecision.

See the tragedy of uncontrolled feeling in the life of David's son, Amnon (2 Samuel 13). First he 'fell in love with Tamar, the beautiful sister of Absalom' (v1). A slave to his own passion, he eventually raped her (v14). Then his emotions did a rapid turnabout:

> 'Then Amnon hated her with _____ _____ .
> In fact, he _____ her more than he had _____ her.'
> (2 Samuel 13:15)

In the end, Amnon's failure to control his feelings led to his own violent death (v28-29, 32).

b. Unsociability

A man who is the prey to his own emotions will find few friends. Who wants to get near a man prone to moodiness, explosions of temper and unpredictable 'highs'?

c. Sickness

Emotional states and bodily functions are closely related. Anxiety can put

51

you off your food. Worry can bring you out in a rash. Christian doctors have frequently noted the connection between, say, anger and glaucoma, or resentment and arthritis, or brooding and stomach ulcers.

> 'A heart at peace gives _____ to the body, but _____
> _____ _____ _____ .'
>
> (Proverbs 14:30)

Healthy, Christlike emotions are a source of physical well-being but ungodly, sin-provoked emotions attack good health. Read Psalm 32:1-5 and see how David's sin affected his health. Notice that confession and forgiveness made him feel 'blessed', i.e. happy.

d. A seared conscience

Strong *negative* emotions are like the red light on a car's dashboard – a sign that something is wrong. To ignore our conscience or attempt to stifle it with tranquillisers is no answer; it is like ignoring the red light or taking the bulb out! This is the quickest route to a seared (i.e. insensitive) conscience. Paul, in warning against dangerous teachings in the church, observed:

> 'Such teachings come through hypocritical liars, whose consciences have been _____ as with a _____
> _____ .'
>
> (1 Timothy 4:2)

Take note of negative emotions, then. Deal with the negative, sinful *behaviour* that has caused them. Not to control them this way is a recipe for disaster. Who, after all, wants to become a 'hypocritical liar'?

5. Controlling Your Feelings

By control we do not mean suppression. To *blow up* with anger is clearly wrong but to *clam up*, keeping the anger inside, is just as wrong. *Im*plosion is no less harmful in the long run than *ex*plosion.

Nor by control do we mean slipping back into the stoical, stiff upper lip approach, or even regarding our emotions as private property. *Good* emotions are to be both *expressed* and *shared*:

'_____ with those who_____ ; _____ with those who _____ .'

(Romans 12:15)

By control we mean *bringing our emotions to a place of proper balance in our lives so that we are men like Jesus*. How can we do this?

a. By imitating the divine emotions

Actively *copy your heavenly Father*, who longs for his children to be like him:

'Be _____ of God, therefore, as dearly loved _____ .'

(Ephesians 5:1)

See from Scripture his active *love*, which reaches out and takes the initiative; his *righteous anger* that burns against sin and injustice; his *compassion* towards the weak and helpless; his *sadness* over man's waywardness and refusal to repent. Cultivate the same emotions yourself.

Notice the feelings that God does *not* have — bitterness and malice, for instance — and eradicate them from your own heart (see Ephesians 4:31).

Actively *copy Christ*. He wept at a graveside, so you can do the same. He denounced hypocrisy in passionately expressed terms; so can you. His face expressed genuine love towards an enquirer whom he probably met only once (Mark 10:21); so can yours. He was the manliest of all men and his emotional life was rich. Imitate him with confidence.

b. By the renewing of the mind

Before we were saved, our thought-patterns were those of the world. Now, however, we are in a new kingdom and our thought-life needs to be gradually renewed so that we think the way God thinks:

53

*'Do not conform any longer to the pattern of this world, but be
_____ by the _____ ____ _____
_____ . Then you will be able to test and approve what God's
will is — his good, pleasing and perfect will.'*

(Romans 12:2)

How we *think* governs the way we *feel*. If, therefore, we are to be men of
God we must think God's thoughts. That way, 'God's will' regarding our
emotional development — 'his good, pleasing and perfect will' — will
become clear. Soak yourself, then, in the Scriptures until your thinking is
renewed.

Here's an example. As you feed on the Word of God, you will become
increasingly aware of God's *hatred for sin*. What the world writes off as
unimportant — 'nobody's perfect', 'it's a white lie' or 'everybody's doing it'
— you will come to hate as God hates. The things that break God's heart
will begin to break yours, and in your emotional life you will come to
appreciate what Jesus meant when he said: 'Blessed are those who mourn'
(Matthew 5:4).

c. By active obedience to the Lord

Every man wants to be happy. As we saw earlier in this lesson, happiness
is not something intangible that merely comes and goes. Nor is it dependent
on circumstances. Happiness comes chiefly from *doing what is right*, and
that is something we can *choose* to do. To a large degree, therefore,
happiness lies within our own control.

Jesus was the *happiest* man who ever lived, because he was the most
righteous:

*'About the Son he says, . . . "You have loved _____ .
and hated _____ ; therefore God, your God, has
set you above your companions by anointing you with the oil
of _____ ." '*

(Hebrews 1:8-9)

True joy will be yours, too, in proportion to your active hatred of wickedness
and your active love of righteousness.

Feelings without Shame: Emotional freedom

Doctors have shown that there are two sides to our nervous system. One side is the involuntary side: it is linked to our bodily glands and organs; it is subject to a variety of emotions that seem to come and go as they please; and it is outside our immediate control. The other side is within our control. It is to do with our minds, our wills and what we do with our bodies. It is the *behaviour* side.

In this latter area we *can* make changes. As we do what is right here, there is a knock-on effect into the other area — that of the emotions. *Right actions*, in other words, produce *right emotions*!

> *'Whoever of you loves life and desires to see _____ _____*
> *_____ , keep your tongue from evil and your lips from*
> *speaking lies. Turn from evil and ____ _____ ; seek peace and*
> *pursue it.'*
>
> (Psalm 34:12-14)

Whenever you 'do good' you will have one of those 'good days'. Doing good, acting rightly, is an intensely personal business. For you it might mean: get out of the armchair and help your wife in the kitchen; list all the jobs you have to do and get started; check your current financial situation to see that you are still 'in the black'; go to the meeting, even though you don't feel like it; ask Bill's forgiveness for your cutting words to him.

'Do whatever he tells you' (John 2:5) is the key to emotional miracles no less amazing than the changing of water into wine. How about it?

* *

55

LESSON 4

Feelings Without Shame: Emotional freedom

True or False

1. T F A man's emotions have their origin in God, who made man in his own image.

2. T F Jesus, the perfect man, never cried.

3. T F Anger is always wrong because Jesus was never angry.

4. T F Temperamentally, some men are more emotional than others.

5. T F Depression can be caused by anticlimax after a period of high emotional concentration.

6. T F Uncontrolled emotion always brings problems.

7. T F A healthy emotional life leads to physical well-being.

8. T F For a man to explode with anger is wrong, but for him to keep his anger inside is just as harmful.

9. T F To copy God's emotions is impossible, so there is no point in trying.

10. T F A man is most joyful when he is most righteous because right feelings come from right actions.

Group Discussion

1. How can parents bring up their sons to have a balanced and healthy emotional life?

2.   How do people react to:

-     a man who never shows any emotion at all?

-     a man who is over-emotional?

Say honestly which of the two extremes you tend towards.

3.   What is the biblical way to handle anger? Is anger always sinful? In addition to the references given under 2a and 2b in this lesson, the following verses will prove helpful:

Ephesians 4:26,31

Proverbs 29:11,22

Matthew 5:22-24; 18:15-17

Personal Assignment

1.   When did tears last fill your eyes in public? How long is it since you said to another person: 'I love you'? When did you last feel *righteous* anger? What do the answers to these questions tell you about the adjustments needed in your emotional development?

2.   Depression affects men as well as women. How do you tackle it in yourself or how would you help another man who is depressed? Note down the scriptural principles that are relevant and show how they apply.

True or False

1.T 2.F 3.F 4.T 5.T 6.T 7.T 8.T 9.F 10.T

LESSON 5

School OF THE
WORD

The Buck Stops Here: Leadership and Responsibility

Harry S. Truman, a former president of USA, is said to have had on his desk a sign declaring: 'The buck stops here.' A buck was originally the marker used to indicate the dealer in a poker game. To 'pass the buck', therefore, came to mean to shift the responsibility on to someone else. Mr Truman realised that, being at the top of the governmental system, he could not pass on responsibility for major decisions to someone further up. Hence: 'The buck stops here'.

One of the marks of a man is a *willingness to take responsibility and exercise leadership*. Truman knew this, and so does every 'true man' today!

1. We Are All Leaders

The original mandate given to Adam and Eve to exercise dominion over the created world extends to both men and women. They are co-regents in their rule. In other respects, however, their rule differs:

a. The social order

'For Adam no suitable helper was found' among the animal creation (Genesis 2:20). God therefore put him to sleep, took a rib and from it formed Eve, 'and he brought her to the man' (v22). The woman was brought to the man to be his 'helper', and so the marriage bond was instituted:

> *'For this reason a man will leave his father and mother and be*
> _____ *to his wife, and they will become* _____
> _____ *.'*

(Genesis 2:24)

With the Fall, that original human relationship was soured. Eve began to want to dominate Adam. This is probably what God meant when, outlining the consequences of the Fall, he said to her: 'Your desire will be for your husband' (Genesis 3:16). 'Desire' is the word also used in Genesis 4:7 for sin's desire to master Cain — an ungodly desire. But, says the Lord to Eve, '*he* will rule over *you*' (Genesis 3:16).

Marriage is God's will for the great majority of people, and within that relationship the man is called to exercise the responsibility of leadership. Paul summarises the situation like this:

> *'The woman is the glory of man. For man did not come from woman, but woman from man; neither was man created for woman, but woman for man.'*

(1 Corinthians 11:7-9)

In the context of marriage, therefore, the command is:

> *'Wives,* _____ *to your* _____ *as to the Lord.*
> *For the husband is the* _____ ____ _____ _____ *as Christ*
> *is the head of the church, his body, of which he is the Saviour.*
> *Now as the church submits to Christ, so also* _____
> _____ _____ ____ _____ _____ *in*
> *everything.'*

(Ephesians 5:22-24)

It is not that the wife is in any way *inferior*; she is not. It is just that, in the divine social order, she is to be *subordinate*.

The fact is that it is often as difficult for the husband to lead as it is for the wife to be submissive. For a successful marriage the man must give his wife something to submit *to*! In this respect the great majority of men are called to be leaders.

60

b. Initiators and implementers

Some men are 'ideas men', naturally taking initiatives and setting out proposals. Other men are more at home taking up these ideas and putting them into practice — implementers rather than initiators.

In practice we are all a mixture of the two. Every man has at least *some* initiative potential and must learn to develop it — in his work, his specialism, his skill or his gift area.

Did your mother run after you, waiting on you hand and foot? Are you (if now married) expecting your wife to do the same? Who handles the family bills? Who plans holidays? Who heads up the decision-making process in the family? It should be you!

Have you turned down promotion in your job because 'I don't want the responsibility and, besides, I don't want to lose the friendship of my workmates'? Then it's time to start being a real man — a man like God, a leader, an initiator, a grasper of responsibility.

2. Essentials for Leadership

a. A servant's heart

Taking responsibility and exercising leadership does not mean pushing other people around. Only a man *under* authority, one who gladly serves others, is qualified to be *in* authority. (See Matthew 8:5-10.) Jesus taught:

> *'You know that the rulers of the Gentiles lord it over them, and their high officials exercise authority over them. Not so with you. Instead, whoever wants to _____ _____ among you must be your _____ , and whoever wants to be _____ must be your _____ — just as the Son of Man did not come to ____ _____ , but to _____ , and to give his life as a ransom for many.'*
>
> (Matthew 20:25-28)

61

How great is your serving capacity? Jesus, the greatest of all men, the ultimate man, gladly washed feet — the most menial task of his day. Can you stoop to lowly tasks? Can you take orders at work? Do you regard certain jobs as beneath you? Stoop low to become a man of leadership. (See Luke 11:10-12.)

b. Willingness to learn from others

Leadership means being humble enough to receive advice, not only from your peers, but also from people less experienced than yourself. Pride will isolate you; humility will endear you to all you meet.

> 'The way of a fool seems right to him, but a _____ man
> _____ ____ _____ .'

(Proverbs 12:15)

c. Being an example

In the Bible, leadership is always exercised by *the power of example*. People will copy what you *are* and *do* rather than fall in with what you merely *say*.

> 'The kingdom of God is not a matter of _____ but of
> _____ .'

(1 Corinthians 4:20)

A real man will exercise his 'kingdom' (i.e. his rule, his leadership) by saying with Gideon: 'Watch me . . . . Follow my lead . . . do exactly as I do' (Judges 7:17). Like Paul, he will say:

> 'Follow _____ _____ , as I follow the example of
> _____ .'

(1 Corinthians 11:1)

Can you confidently say this to your family, your juniors at work, your dependants? A real man practises what he preaches and preaches only what he practises.

d. Godly confidence

Even though painfully aware of your shortcomings, anticipate success! God never calls us to responsibilities without giving us the strength we need. In fact, 'his divine power has given us *everything we need* for life and godliness' (2 Peter 1:3), so the only thing we can't do is say, 'I can't!'

> 'I _____ do _____ *through him who gives me strength.'*
>
> (Philippians 4:13)

You will never be a real man until you believe the truth of God's ability to make you one!

3. Leadership Attitudes

a. Seriousness

A real man is serious without being overly solemn. Certainly he will be able to laugh and enjoy a joke, but he will not play the permanent jester, for a man whose every word is a jest will never win the confidence of others in things that matter. They know that life is not one big joke and will not trust a man who acts as if it is.

> *'The tongue of the wise commends knowledge, but the mouth of the fool _____ _____ .'*
>
> (Proverbs 15:2)

b. Acceptance of responsibility

1. For your successes

Can you receive compliments graciously? Or do you say:

– 'Oh, it wasn't me, it was all the Lord.' This is rarely true; it is you, your effort or skill, your partnership with him that is being complimented. Accept it.

- *'It could have been much better.'* This is an ungracious slap in the face to your complimenter. You are really saying: 'If you thought my performance was good it doesn't say much for your judgment.'

- *Some inane or half-embarrassed remark.* This in turn embarrasses the one who has made the compliment and robs you of manly integrity in his sight.

Far better to acknowledge the compliment with: 'Thank you' or: 'It's nice of you to say so' or: 'I appreciate your encouragement very much.'

2. For your failures

The instinct to dodge responsibility for our sins and failures goes right back to Eden. When God confronted Adam about eating the forbidden fruit, the blame was passed down the line to Eve and on to the serpent:

> *'The man said, "The _____ you put here with me — _____ gave me some fruit from the tree, and I ate it." Then the Lord God said to the woman, "What is this you have done?" The woman said, "The _____ deceived me, and I ate." '*
> (Genesis 3:12-13)

Such blame-shifting has no place in the life of a man of God. We must accept responsibility. David was 'a man after God's own heart' — the kind of man we all want to be. When confronted by Nathan over his adultery with Bathsheba, he openly admitted: 'I have sinned against the Lord' (2 Samuel 12:13). The prodigal, too, freely confessed to his own father: 'I have sinned against heaven and against you' (Luke 15:21). That's being a man!

3. For your God-given tasks

The world is crying out for men who will take their responsibilities seriously. Have you a wife and children? Then be active in taking responsibility for them; don't let things drift. Have you a job? Then work at it responsibly, without the need for your boss to watch you all the time.

One day each of us must answer to God according to the responsibilities given to us (Romans 14:12). Each man's work —

*. . . will be shown for what it is, because the Day will bring it to light. It will be revealed with fire, and the fire will test _____
_____ ___ _____ _____ _____ .'*

(1 Corinthians 3:13)

c. Initiative

To be a man of God is to be a man of initiative, for God takes initiatives. He it was who said: 'Let there be' and: 'Let us make' at the *creation*. He took the initiative, too, in *salvation*. We were 'dead in . . . transgressions and sins' and 'by nature objects of wrath' (Ephesians 2:1,3). Then:

'Because of his great love for us, _____ who is rich in mercy, _____ ___ _____ with Christ even when we were dead in transgressions — it is by _____ you have been saved.'
(Ephesians 2:4-5)

We men must learn to take initiative, to make the first move to change things, for we are made in God's image. 'Don't wait for something to turn up,' said one wise man. 'Go and turn up something!' Let's not adapt to the status quo; as men of God let's change it for the better.

d. Courage

To be cautious is wise, but to be *over*-cautious is unmanly. Courage, or boldness, is a manly virtue that was urged upon (among others) Joshua (Joshua 1:6,9), Solomon (1 Chronicles 22:13), good King Asa (2 Chronicles 15:7) and the judges appointed by Jehoshaphat (2 Chronicles 19:11). To the men of Corinth Paul stated:

'Be on your guard; stand firm in the faith; be _____ ___ _____ ; be _____ .'
(1 Corinthians 16:13)

Courage is compatible with fear. In spite of your thumping heart and dry mouth, step out and do what has to be done.

Sometimes it is *physical* courage that is required (rescuing someone from a burning house). More often it will be the courage of your *convictions* (telling

65

the boss you will not be a party to fiddling the office accounts).

Women can also be courageous, though in them it tends to be *protective*, as when a mother will defend her children to the death. In men courage is usually more *aggressive*, in keeping with man's thrusting nature. Are you a man of courage? If not you can be, provided you are a righteous man, for:

> 'The wicked man flees though no-one pursues, but the righteous are ____ _____ ____ __ _____ .'
>
> (Proverbs 28:1)

4. Exercising Leadership

So far we have looked at those aspects of leadership, initiative and the taking of responsibility that should be the marks of *every* man.

To conclude this lesson we will consider a few simple guidelines to help you in specific areas of leadership — where you have responsibility for and authority over other people in the realm of family, work or church.

a. Plan ahead and set goals

Goals should be both long-term and short-term, *like the ones God gave Abraham*. Long-term, God said:

> 'I will make you into a _____ _____ . . . and all peoples on earth will be blessed through you.'
>
> (Genesis 12:2-3)

Elderly and childless, Abraham must have found this quite staggering. The short-term goal doubtless brought things more within his grasp: 'Sarah your wife will have a *son*' (Genesis 18:10).

Set both long- and short-term goals for your dependants (a career in medicine; a holiday in the sun next year) and be open to course changes en route.

b. Listen to your dependants

You may make final decisions, but your dependants have views and opinions to which they need to know you have listened with care. After all, their information and insights may affect your final decision.

Notice how wisely *James* handled the *Council of Jerusalem* in Acts 15:6-20. After 'much discussion' (v7) and speeches by several main speakers, he was able to sum up confidently by saying: 'It is *my* judgment, therefore, that . . .'(v19). Be a careful listener and your dependants will trust your judgment.

c. Set guidelines for your dependants

Lay out the basic requirements, but then *leave them room to manoeuvre* and to make personal decisions within the general scheme. This will enable them to exercise initiative, find fulfilment and develop their own leadership skills.

Read Genesis 24 and see how *Abraham took this approach with his chief servant* over the matter of getting a wife for Isaac. The task was set (v2-4), the servant's queries were answered (v5-8), and Abraham then left him to it. The results were first class!

d. Inspect your dependants' work and progress

They need to know that you are still interested and taking note of what they are doing. Where necessary, *confront them* with their failures, even if you are going to be disliked for it.

Nobody exercising leadership can please all the people all the time. It is the mark of a man, however, that he doesn't need to be liked; it is enough for him to know that he is respected.

This is how Paul handled his converts in the young churches:

> *'We proclaim [Christ],* _____ *and* _____
> *everyone with all wisdom, so that we may present everyone*
> _____ *[i.e. complete, mature] in Christ.'*
>
> (Colossians 1:28)

That word 'admonishing' means confronting them, facing them up with areas of weakness. Are you man enough to do it, and to do it in an acceptable manner?

e. Be an encourager

In your leadership role, whatever it may be, give encouragement whenever you can. That way, you are like your Father, who is called 'a God of every consolation and encouragement' (2 Corinthians 1:3 Wuest).

Think what it must have meant to Jesus when God publicly proclaimed:

> 'You are my Son, whom I love; with you I am _____
> _____ .'

(Luke 3:22)

When did you last say something like that to one of your dependants? Be encouraged to be an encourager!

* *

LESSON 5

The Buck Stops Here: Leadership and responsibility

True or False

1. T F It is often as difficult for a husband to lead as it is for his wife to be submissive.

2. T F Some men are implementers rather than initiators but even they are called to take initiative.

3. T F Only a man under authority can legitimately exercise authority over others.

4. T F A real man is always willing to learn, even from people younger or less experienced than himself.

5. T F We lead chiefly by the power of example.

6. T F As men we should never admit our mistakes; we should try to explain them away.

7. T F Rather than wait for something to turn up, a man should go and turn up something.

8. T F Courage and fear cannot exist together.

9. T F Leadership means shouting down your dependants and asserting your own ideas.

10. T F Every true man must learn the art of godly confrontation.

Group Discussion

1. Why is it so easy to opt out of leadership and let things drift, especially in the family situation?

2. Radio and TV (especially comedy programmes) habitually portray men who are childish, bungling and stupid. They are pushed around by the women in their lives and are little more than grown-up schoolboys. How does this caricature reflect the spirit of the age? Are men really like that?

3. Talk frankly with a view to identifying areas of life where your leadership and responsibility need to be taken more seriously. Avoid being vague; give practical examples.

Personal Assignment

1. List the areas in which you currently have a God-given leadership responsibility — family, job, church, etc. Try to put yourself in the shoes of your dependants or those looking on, and assess the quality of your leadership from their point of view.

2. When did you last:

    – review your situation?

    – confront someone?

    – give encouragement?

    – take a 'faith risk'?

    Identify specific actions you need to take or new patterns of responsibility to implement. Then get started!

True or False

1.T 2.T 3.T 4.T 5.T 6.F 7.T 8.F 9.F 10.T

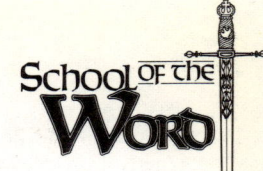

School OF THE
Word

Strength with Kindness: Attitudes to women

'Why can't a woman be just like a man?' asks Professor Higgins in *My Fair Lady*. The answer is simple: if she were just like a man she would no longer be a woman at all! Men and women just *are* different. God fixed it that way. And we can all sympathise with the classic French reaction: '*Vive la différence*!'

Jesus got on well with womankind, even though he remained single for the kingdom's sake. Of all the gospel writers, Luke is the one who highlights this aspect of his life.

Since half the world's population is female, a man who can't get on with women is seriously handicapped in his social life. In this lesson, therefore, we explain the question of our attitude to women. Let's begin with our relationship to the first woman we ever met — mother.

1. Mother — Our First Lady

a. She is to be honoured

Father may be the head of the family, but the commandment to 'honour' extends to both parents. And there is a *promise* attached:

> ' "*Honour your father* _____ _____ " — *which is the first commandment with a promise* — "*that it may ____ _____ with you and that you may enjoy _____ _____ on the earth.*" '

> (Ephesians 6:2-3)

71

Whether she is a believer or not is irrelevant. Unless you want a life of problems followed by an early death, honour your mother. 'A foolish man despises his mother' (Proverbs 15:20). Now you know why!

Honour includes *obedience* during the time we are young, living at home and under her care. God views disobedience to mothers very gravely indeed. (See Proverbs 30:17.) Such disobedience is a feature of that empty powerless Christianity which some will profess in the last days (2 Timothy 3:1-5).

b. Honour extends into old age

Honour also includes *respect*. Even if there is little to respect in her character and attitude, you must show due respect to your mother *just because she is your mother*.

This is easy to let slip when she becomes weak and dependent with old age:

'Do not despise your mother _____ _____ ____ _____ .'
(Proverbs 23:22)

c. The example of Jesus

Jesus honoured his mother, Mary, at all times. Even when racked with pain on the cross he gave attention to her needs, entrusting her to the care of John. (See John 19:25-27.)

When actively involved, as a grown man, in his public ministry, Jesus didn't allow himself to be pressured by his mother and her demands (Matthew 12:46-50), yet he clearly loved and honoured her. As a grown man, you too can honour your mother without allowing her to restrict your work or your movements.

2. Sisters — Not to be Neglected

Boys in a family have a tendency to look down on their sisters and treat them as 'mere girls', especially if they are younger. Sometimes this attitude can persist into adulthood.

In God's purpose, the family is the *nursery of human relationships*. If you never learn to treat your sisters with a right attitude of *love, encouragement* and *protectiveness*, you will have problems treating women in general that way.

Mother and sisters are inextricably linked by their womanhood. A man who mistreats his mother is hardly going to treat his sisters properly, and his treatment of both will in due course extend to other women. The way a young man treats his mother, for example, is the way he will treat his wife when he gets one.

3. Women in General

a. In the world

1. Treat all women with great respect

Treat women with respect, just as Jesus did. He never looked down on them, ridiculed them or walked roughshod over their feelings.

He was understanding and patient. He was a good *listener*. Notice how he dealt with the Samaritan woman in John 4. Even though she was of dubious moral character he treated her with the utmost respect.

> *'The fruit of the Spirit is love, joy, peace, patience, kindness, goodness, faithfulness, _____ and self-control.'*
> (Galatians 5:22-23)

Here is one aspect of the Spirit's fruit that a man should develop in his relationships with women at every level. Gentleness here is 'the opposite to self-assertiveness and self-interest' (W.E. Vine). It is being warm and considerate, qualities which flow from security in God and a reserve of inner power. The man who, by contrast, is pushy and self-assertive towards women is no real *gentle*man at all.

2. Avoid flirting at all costs

A man can 'catch' almost any woman if he really wants to. Though you may be tempted to put your skill to the test in this respect by flirting, resist it vigorously. Make up your mind never to start that process of meaningful looks, hint-loaded conversation and touch which plays with man-woman attraction without godly intention.

If ever you are sexually accosted by a woman, do what Joseph did — *refuse adamantly*. He said to Potiphar's wife, who was attempting to seduce him:

> ' *"How then could I do such a wicked thing and* _____ _____
> _____ *?" And though she spoke to Joseph day after day, he*
> _____ *to go to bed with her or* _____ ___ _____
> _____ .'

> (Genesis 39:9-10)

If necessary, follow Joseph's example and *run away* (v12). That's not weakness; it's a sign of spiritual strength and sound common sense.

b. In the church

All the above applies in the church, and to it we can add Paul's exhortation to the young man Timothy:

> 'Treat younger men as brothers, older women as _____ ,
> and younger women as _____ , with absolute
> _____ .'

> (1 Timothy 5:1-2)

1. The holy kiss

'Greet one another with a *holy kiss*' (Romans 16:16) is Paul's word to the churches. Western culture caused J.B. Phillips to translate this verse (and similar ones in other letters): 'Give each other a hearty handshake all round'!

In recent times, however, the holy kiss or Christian embrace has again become common. Exercised *with care*, especially towards sisters in the Lord, it helps God's people avoid two extremes:

- the overtly sexual touching of a permissive society.

- the starchy 'no touching' attitude which has so often in the past caused a feeling of physical isolation.

2. The counselling question

Should men counsel women?

> 'Do not rebuke an older man, but **exhort** him as a father, the younger men as brothers, the **older women** as mothers, the **younger** as sisters, with all purity.'
>
> (1 Timothy 5:1-2 RAV)

The word *exhort* here, addressed to Timothy, appears to refer to personal confrontation or counselling and, in the Greek, extends to both older and younger women. Such counselling is best done, however, with a third party present, to prevent the kind of impropriety which could easily develop in an intense counselling situation. Certainly the one man/one woman situation is best avoided.

4. Potential Wives

a. Mixing widely

Single young men should mix widely with other singles of both sexes. It is in this kind of broad fellowship that a young man can best meet a possible future partner.

Here is an ideal opportunity for *male initiative*: the arranging of meetings and social occasions where this wide fellowshipping can take place.

b. Asking a girl out

In Bible times it was customary for parents to arrange marriages for their children, even though the attraction between two young people themselves might well have been the starting point.

> 'Samson went down to Timnah and saw there a young Philistine
> woman. When he returned, he said to his father and mother, "I
> have seen a Philistine woman in Timnah; now _____ _____
> _____ ____ as my wife." '

(Judges 14:1-2)

Parents today tend not to be involved in the same way. But the initiative in courtship is still viewed as lying with the young man. This does not rule out the right of a girl to make her feelings known, as Ruth illustrates (Ruth 2:1 — 4:13, especially 3:1-9), though there were the special circumstances of the kinsman-redeemer and levirate marriage in her situation (which a commentary on the book of Ruth will explain).

A young man should not:

— adopt an over-casual approach by deliberately taking out a whole series of girls in turn.

— expect the Lord to say: 'This is the girl to marry' before even asking her out. This approach is likely to prove unreal and superspiritual.

In taking a girl out and getting to know her better, he should be *sensitive to her feelings*. Knowing that, as Byron said:

> 'Man's love is of man's life a thing apart,
> 'Tis woman's whole existence,'

he will not raise her expectations prematurely by talking too soon about the prospect of marriage.

c. Breaking it off

Once it becomes clear that such a friendship is not to end in engagement and marriage, it should be terminated. Don't do it by letter. This only documents the situation, providing a permanent platform for the girl's grief. Do if *face to face*.

Build the girl up. Her self-esteem will have taken a heavy blow, so leave her with something to hold on to by assuring her that you are the richer for having got to know her. Then pray with her, committing your individual futures to the Lord.

5. Steady Girlfriend or Fiancée

a. Take the lead

Begin to establish *now* the pattern of relationship that will mark your eventual marriage:

> *'The husband is* _____ _____ *of the wife as Christ is the head of the church.'*
>
> (Ephesians 5:23)

Take the lead in a kind and self-sacrificial way. Instinctively a woman *wants* to be led this way:

> **'Draw me** after you and let us run together!'
>
> (Song of Solomon 1:4 NASB)

b. Keep the sexual urge under control

In lesson 3, section b, we saw the importance of sexual restraint. During engagement (which is best kept short) this can be a particular pressure. Since you are 'promised' to each other there is temptation to anticipate the marriage.

Don't yield to this urge. Take the lead in avoiding stirring up strong desires which cannot legitimately be satisfied until after the wedding. The best way to do this is by frank communication and keeping the spiritual dimension of your relationship uppermost:

> *'Live by the* _____ *, and you will not* _____ *the* _____ *of the flesh.'*
>
> (Galatians 5:16 margin)

Be a man of principle in this respect and your eventual marriage will benefit immensely.

77

c. See her as a whole person

She has a mind, interests and opinions as well as a body. Therefore:

1. Don't treat her as a plaything

She is a real, whole person, not just a 'living doll'.

2. Don't idolise her

The 'I'm not worthy of you' approach produces self-deprecation, failure to give the proper lead and a tendency to give her whatever she wants (which means that, in practice, *she* leads).

d. Recognise your differences

You and she are different, not just because you are two individuals but because she is a woman and you are a man. A woman's major needs include:

1. Security

This is a security that can best be found in a caring man — father or husband — who exercises responsible leadership.

2. Emotional expression

A woman needs to express her feelings, which play a larger part in her life than in a man's. A man tends to be more matter-of-fact and calculating.

A woman often does not understand *why* she feels as she does. Also, her monthly cycle and the accompanying hormonal changes can strongly affect her emotions, causing her, for example, to burst into tears for no apparent reason. At such times she needs not explanations or analysis but tender love and understanding. The wise man provides it.

3. Romance

Most men don't really know what romance is! But they can learn — and provide it. It includes *atmosphere*, which you can create with, say, candlelight and nice surroundings. It includes *adventure* — taking her somewhere new or engaging in some novel activity. It includes *extravagance*. Without being irresponsible, you should occasionally buy and give her something that normally you wouldn't dream of purchasing, something non-essential, something luxurious. It includes *surprises*. Predictability and routine can be wearying at times; a pleasant surprise can bring instant refreshment. Organise one!

4. Communication

Many a man has been baffled by the words: 'Talk to me!' Don't try to understand it; just do it. In particular, tell her how you *feel* about her, about your relationship, about life, about circumstances.

6. Wife

a. Love her

> *'Husbands, _____ _____ _____ , just as Christ loved the church and _____ _____ _____ for her to make her holy, cleansing her by the washing with water through the word, and to _____ her to himself as a _____ church.'*

(Ephesians 5:25-27)

'*Love* your wives' is a *command*. It does not, therefore, refer to feelings or the sexual urge which, by their very nature, are not subject to commands.

Paul makes it clear in the above Scripture that 'love' here is what was exemplified by Jesus in his love for his bride, the church: He 'gave himself up for her' (v25). Husbandly love, therefore, is to be *self-sacrificial*. It means putting your interests second and hers first! Are you, in the light of this, a truly loving husband?

b. Be faithful to her

In your marriage vows you probably said something like 'till death us do part' or 'as long as we both shall live' to underscore your intention to be faithful. This means:

1. No adultery

That includes both the deed and the thought:

> *'Marriage should be honoured by all, and the marriage bed*
> _____ _____ *, for God will* _____ _____
> _____ *and all the sexually immoral.'*
>
> (Hebrews 13:4)

Note that this is a New Testament verse, addressed to believers.

2. No divorce

Don't let the possibility of divorce even enter your head. Jesus said:

> *'Anyone who divorces his wife, except for marital unfaithfulness, and marries another woman commits adultery.'*
>
> (Matthew 19:9)

And even if your wife *is* unfaithful, you don't *have* to divorce her; you could forgive her and rebuild the relationship. Better, however, to put divorce right out of your mind and work at a lasting and ever-improving marriage.

c. Put her before the children

There is a clear order in Scripture for Christian husbands:

> *'Whatever you do, whether in word or deed, do it all in the*
> _____ ____ _____ _____ _____ *, giving thanks to*
> *God the Father through him . . . . Husbands, love* _____
> _____ *and do not be harsh with them . . . . Fathers, do not*
> *embitter* _____ _____ *, or they will become*
> *discouraged.'*
>
> (Colossians 3:17, 19, 21)

The order is: (i) the Lord; (ii) your wife; (iii) your children. The same order is apparent in Ephesians 5:20 — 6:4. When a man puts his children before his wife he sows the seeds of family chaos. See how Isaac and Rebekah caused lasting trouble for themselves this way in Genesis 27.

d. Praise her

A wife responds strongly to words of praise and appreciation. Don't be content to tell her (as you often should) that you love her. Commend her in particular areas.

> *'Her children arise and call her blessed; her* _____
> *also, and he* _____ *her: "Many women do noble things, but*
> *you* _____ _____ _____ *." '*
>
> (Proverbs 31:28-29)

Why do the children in this Bible passage so naturally praise their mother? Doubtless because their father has frequently praised her *in their presence* and they are following his example. When did you last praise your wife?

7. What Women Appreciate

By way of summary, the following are the qualities that women tend to appreciate most in a man. Whether married or not, you can measure your manhood in relation to womankind against this list.

Where you find yourself lacking, let faith and holy determination reach to God to make up the deficiency:

– *leadership*: taking initiative, accepting responsibility, being decisive.

– *consistency*: being reliable, trustworthy and (in the best sense) predictable.

– *emotional stability*: not moody or prone to strong ups and downs.

– *tenderness*: strength tempered with gentleness and caring; power under control.

– *ambition*: not sitting back and letting life happen, but taking it in hand and shaping it.

LESSON 6

Strength with Kindness: Attitudes to women

True or False

1. T F Mothers are to be honoured, even in weakness and old age.

2. T F Sisters are inferior and to be treated with condescension.

3. T F Jesus found women difficult to get on with.

4. T F To run away from an openly seductive woman is a sign of wisdom and strength of character.

5. T F One man/one woman counselling is a spiritual business and holds no dangers.

6. T F Single men should avoid both casual romances and superspiritual notions of finding the right partner.

7. T F The best way to control the desires of the flesh is to live by the Holy Spirit.

8. T F How to meet a woman's need for romance is something a man can learn.

9. T F The kind of love husbands are commanded to show their wives is self-sacrificial love.

10. T F A man should often praise his wife in the presence of their children.

Group Discussion

1.   It has been said that 'when God took Adam's rib to make Eve, what he really took was Adam's radar set'. Woman, in other words, has an *intuition* and *sensitivity* which most men lack. Discuss how this shows in practice. Give examples from experience.

2.   What is the world's view of what a man should be in relation to women? What are the main differences between that view and the scriptural view, especially the example of Jesus?

3.   'A man is attracted primarily by a woman's *appearance*; a woman, however, is drawn first to a man's *manner and character*.' What misunderstandings have commonly arisen from our failure to grasp this fact? Give examples.

Personal Assignment

1.   Review your relationship with your mother and sisters. Are there past failings to seek their forgiveness for? Or present changes to make? Act accordingly.

2.   List the new understandings about women that you have gained from this study. What steps can you take to ensure that you don't let them slip?

3.   Look at the qualities listed in section 7 of this lesson. Notice how they fit in with the picture of Christian manhood built up in previous lessons. See them as yet another incentive to become a real man.

True or False

1.T 2.F 3.F 4.T 5.F 6.T 7.T 8.T 9.T 10.T

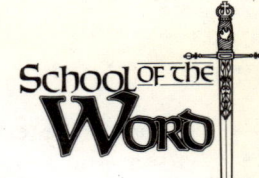

School OF THE
WORD

Something to Show: Work and productivity

The whole question of work is beset with misunderstandings. Some men, as they labour at their jobs, mutter: 'It's all Adam's fault', seeing work as a necessary evil in consequence of the Fall. Others believe that the main purpose in working is to reach a stage of material well-being where work is no longer necessary. Endless leisure is their goal.

Since, for most of us, at least one third of every twenty-four-hour period is taken up with work, it is vital that we have a right attitude towards it. Our manhood is bound up with our view of work and, as always, the Word of God must be our guide.

1. Work is Necessary

a. As part of God's perfect plan

God himself is a worker:

> 'By the seventh day God had finished the **work** he had been doing; so on the seventh day he rested from all his **work**.'
>
> (Genesis 2:2)

He is working still (John 5:17). Man, whom God made in his own image, is designed to be a worker, and *even before the Fall* he was given work responsibility by which he could glorify God:

> *'The Lord God took the man and put him in the Garden of Eden to _____ ____ and _____ _____ of it.'*
>
> (Genesis 2:15)

Certainly after the Fall work became tougher going. 'By the sweat of your brow you will eat your food' was to be the lot of Adam and his descendants (Genesis 3:19).

Work can be redeemed in Christ, however, and become a means of glorifying God. And even though it takes place in a fallen world, it becomes for the Christian a primary outworking of *God's will* for him. It was to Christian slaves, regarding their attitude to their masters, that Paul said:

> *'Obey them not only to win their favour when their eye is on you, but like slaves of Christ, doing _____ _____ ____ _____ from your heart.'*

> (Ephesians 6:6)

b. For self-acceptance in the man's role

While the woman's role is chiefly to be a childbearer and homemaker (though not exclusively, as we shall see), the man's is to be the *breadwinner*. His is the responsibility to provide for his family:

> *'If anyone does not _____ for his _____ , and especially for his _____ _____ , he has denied the faith and is worse than an unbeliever.'*

> (1 Timothy 5:8)

A man instinctively knows this, and to work for his living gives him *dignity, rule, self-esteem* and *legitimate pride*. He gets great satisfaction and fulfilment from seeing the fruits of his labour — something to show for his work:

> *'The lazy man does not roast his game, but the diligent man _____ his _____ .'*

> (Proverbs 12:27)

'Diligence' here means tackling his work with a will and enthusiasm.

c. To earn one's bread

It is a basic principle of life that *a man should earn his own bread by honest work*. State aid is a privilege, not a right (and, indeed, has certain disadvantages). Nothing should stand in the way of the Christian man's efforts to be gainfully employed — including the awareness of Christ's near return, which, even in Paul's day, was causing some men to neglect their work responsibility:

> *'When we were with you, we gave you this rule: "If a man will not _____ , he shall not _____ ." We hear that some among you are idle. They are not busy; they are busybodies. Such people we command and urge in the Lord Jesus Christ to settle down and _____ _____ _____ _____ _____ .'*
>
> (2 Thessalonians 3:10-12)

d. To help appreciate leisure

Rest, relaxation and leisure lose their appeal when they become permanent. They are appreciated best as a contrast to hard work:

> *'The _____ of a _____ is sweet.'*
> (Ecclesiastes 5:12)

This is why we should not expect permanent leisure in the age to come. Even there we will have work to do. And, amazingly enough, the more diligent we prove to be in our work now, the greater the reward of *more work and responsibility* in the coming age! (See the parable of the minas in Luke 19:11-27.) The Christian man will be keen to get in plenty of practice here and now!

2. Some Important Reminders

a. All work is honourable

We have a tendency to categorise work, seeing 'clean' jobs (in the office, the classroom, the laboratory) as somehow 'better' than 'dirty' jobs (in the field, the workshop, the factory).

Jesus, however, invested with dignity even the most menial of tasks — eastern foot-washing — and sanctified the skilled manual work of carpentry. He called as his disciples both a rough-handed fisherman like Peter and a desk-worker like Matthew. Paul, though trained as a Jewish academic, also practised the craft of tent-making. *All* work is honourable to the Christian man.

87

b. God commands one day's rest in seven

The day of rest was meant to be just that — a day of *rest*, not primarily a day of worship or other Christian activity:

> '*Six days you shall_____ and do all your_____ , but the seventh day is a Sabbath to the Lord your God. On it you shall_____ ____ _____ _____ .*'
>
> (Exodus 20:9-10)

While it is true that, spiritually speaking, Jesus is our Sabbath and we, wearied with our own attempts at earning salvation, have been glad to 'enter that rest' by faith (Hebrews 3:16-4:11), the basic need for one day's rest in seven still remains. It is an ordinance dating from *before* the law of Moses (Genesis 2:2-3) and is God's plan for our personal welfare — physically, mentally and emotionally.

Notice, however, that *six* days are allocated for labour. The Christian man who fills them with work of one kind or another (not necessarily just his usual employment) can most appreciate his day of rest.

c. Think twice about working wives

For a married woman to do paid work over and above her domestic responsibilities is not forbidden. The 'perfect wife' of Proverbs 31 is a working wife (v16-18, 24). Notice, however, that this is not at the expense of her prior loyalties to:

- *God* She 'fears the Lord' (v30).

- *Her husband* She wins his appreciation (v11-12, 28b).

- *Her children* She cares for them (v15, 21, 27-28a).

- *The community* She serves it (v20).

A wise Christian husband will be aware of some of the dangers faced by the family where the wife works full time, especially when there are young children:

- Questionable economics. High tax is usually payable.

- His wife may well look her best at work and her worst at home, where housework can become a pressure. This is obviously bad for the husband-wife relationship.

- Materialistic temptation: 'We don't want children; we like our present double-income life-style too much.'

- Humiliation to the husband if he is not the breadwinner or if his wife has a higher income than his own.

- Possible neglect of the children.

3. What to Avoid in Your Work

a. Striking

One cannot bring a solid biblical case for saying that striking is wrong, but since a strike's immediate effects are invariably negative, disruptive and harmful, this should probably be the very last resort for the Christian worker, whose calling as a believer is to be *constructive*.

Many of the New Testament's exhortations are not to employers and employees, who have a *voluntary* relationship, but to masters and slaves. A slave had no rights at all, least of all the right to withdraw his labour. Nevertheless, these exhortations contain some basic principles applicable to our present-day work scene.

If an opportunity to gain his freedom came up, a slave was urged to take it (1 Corinthians 7:21). Otherwise, the position was:

> *'Slaves, _____ _____ to your masters with all _____ , not only to those who are good and considerate, but also to those who are _____ .'*
>
> (1 Peter 2:18)

Note that submission cannot be forced; it must be voluntary on the worker's part: 'submit *yourselves*'. It does not, however, mean being a doormat. Biblical submission includes the right to express an opinion, question an attitude or voice a legitimate complaint. Hopefully, a Christian attitude in a difficult work situation would normally prompt resolution by means other than striking.

b. Compromise

In a predominantly godless society where self-seeking and dishonesty are rife, the Christian man will often find himself the odd man out at work. Pressure will come upon him to *lower his standards*. Such compromise is, of course, dishonouring to God. Be a man and, with good humour and quiet firmness, insist on sticking to Christian values, even if you are made to suffer for it:

> 'It is _____ if a man bears up under the pain of
> _____ suffering because he is _____ ____
> _____ . But how is it to your credit if you receive a beating for
> doing _____ and endure it? But if you _____ for
> _____ _____ and you endure it, this is commendable
> before God.'
>
> (1 Peter 2:19-20)

Are you man enough to stand for righteousness at work?

c. Deceit

'Look busy, the boss is coming!' is an attitude foreign to Christian men, who are urged to work for their masters:

> '. . . **not only when their eye is on you** and to win their favour,
> but with sincerity of heart and reverence for the Lord'.
>
> (Colossians 3:22)

d. Taking advantage of a Christian boss

The Christian employee working for a Christian boss should not expect to exploit this situation for his own advantage. On the contrary:

> 'Those who have _____ _____ are not
> to show less respect for them because they are brothers. Instead,
> they are to _____ _____ _____ _____ ,
> because those who benefit from their service are believers, and
> dear to them.'
>
> (1 Timothy 6:2)

e. Stealing

The theft of an employer's *goods* (tools, materials, stationery, etc) is clearly 'out' for the Christian worker:

'Teach slaves to be subject to their masters . . . and **not to steal from them**, but to show that they can be fully trusted.'

(Titus 2:9-10)

But stealing can take other forms. By neglecting punctuality you can steal your employer's *time*. By destructive criticism (often disguised as jesting) you can steal his *reputation*. The true Christian man is no thief — in any of these areas!

4. How Christian Men Should Work

a. As if Jesus were the boss — he is!

Would your work attitudes change drastically if Jesus were your boss? If so, listen to Paul:

'*Whatever you do, work at it with all your heart, ____ _____ _____ _____ _____ , not for men, since you know that you will receive an inheritance from the Lord as a reward. It is _____ _____ _____ you are _____ .*'

(Colossians 3:23-24)

The Christian man works not merely as *if* Jesus were the boss. He works knowing that in the final analysis Jesus *is* the boss, as Paul's last sentence makes clear. 'Jesus is Lord' (or Boss) is the hallmark of the believer's practice, and that extends to his work.

b. Wholeheartedly

With Jesus as supervisor, there is only one way a man can do his work: *with all his heart*. Tackle the job with vigour and enthusiasm. If it is boring, devise ways of building a challenge into it. Let no-one be able to say, as they watch you at work, 'His heart isn't in it.' Scripture urges us to work

'*like slaves of Christ, doing the will of God _____ _____ _____ . Serve _____ , as if you were serving the Lord, not men.*'

(Ephesians 6:6-7)

5. Results of a Right Work Attitude

a. The gospel is commended

The biggest hindrance to the acceptance of the gospel by unbelievers is the lives of professing Christians, who often fail to practise what they preach. Some regard witnessing in company time as more important than work, the 'spiritual' taking precedence over the 'secular', then wonder why their fellow-workers (especially the boss) don't get saved!

In Christ, *everything* is spiritual, including work and the way we do it. 'Jesus Christ . . . is Lord of all' (Acts 10:36). Christian men are to serve their employers 'so that God's name and our teaching may not be slandered' (1 Timothy 6:1). By the very way they do their work,

> *'in every way they will make the _____ about God our Saviour _____ :'*
> (Titus 2:10)

Some fellow-workers will, of course, despise the hard worker, misunderstanding his motives. That is part of the price of being a man of God. Provided, however, that good humour and friendliness are kept to the forefront and a 'holier than thou' attitude avoided, God's evident blessing upon you will close their mouths:

> *'It is God's will that by _____ _____ you should silence the ignorant talk of _____ _____ :'*
> (1 Peter 2:15)

b. Prosperity

The psalmist assures us that the man who orders his life according to the law of the Lord will know God's blessing: '*Whatever* he does *prospers*' (Psalm 1:3).

The necessities of life — food, clothing, etc — will be yours, plus more, as you bring God into your work life and see it as being under his kingdom-rule:

> *'Do not worry, saying, "What shall we eat?" or "What shall we drink?" or "What shall we wear?" For the pagans run after all these things, and your heavenly Father knows that you need them. But _____ _____ _____ _____ and his _____ , and all these things will be given to you as well.'*
> (Matthew 6:31-33)

92

c. A reward from God

The Lord himself is your boss, as we have seen, and he will reward you for your work not only here and now but in the age to come:

> 'Whatever you do, work at it with all your heart, as working for the Lord, not for men, since you know that you will receive an _____ from the Lord as a _____ .'
>
> (Colossians 3:23-24)

6. How to Become a Loyal Employee

Loyalty — faithfulness — is in short supply in the world. God wants his men, however, to demonstrate this aspect of the fruit of the Spirit in their work. How can you do it?

a. Kill off your independent attitude

This wrong kind of independence can be seen in:

- competing for the boss's recognition, and being jealous when others are promoted.

- complaining about the changes in your job that he puts forward; inflexibility.

- regarding the whole job just as a temporary step in the working out of your *personal* aspirations.

Watch out for these indicators and seek God's help in reshaping your underlying attitude to one of loyalty.

b. Develop a servant's heart

Consider how you can become a better *servant* to your employer or your company. How?

- by actively looking for ways to increase your efficiency.

- by working hard at every task you are given, especially the ones nobody else wants.

93

– by seeing an awkward boss as a tool in God's hand to bring out spiritual qualities and mature attitudes in you.

c. Look to God to give you work-fulfilment

Because, as we saw earlier, work is part of God's perfect plan for you, he wants you to be fulfilled in it. To have a job suited to your personal skills and abilities is a great blessing, but it is not always possible. You may have to settle for work of a dull or repetitive nature. Either way, you can look to *God* to provide you with maximum fulfilment:

> 'Find rest, O my soul, ____ _____ _____ ; my hope comes from him. ____ _____ is my rock and my salvation; he is my fortress, I shall not be shaken. My salvation and my honour _____ ____ _____ ; he is my mighty rock, my refuge.'
> (Psalm 62:5-7)

Postscript

It is important to distinguish between *work* and *employment*. By employment we mean doing a job for which we are paid. The call of God, however, is to *work*, that is, to constructive and productive effort, whether paid or not.

If, in spite of faithful service to your employer, you find yourself unemployed, remember that:

– God knows and understands, and he is on your side.

– Satan will try to burden you with a sense of guilt. Resist it vigorously; you are not to blame.

– While seeking alternative employment you still need to *work*, that is, to discipline yourself to occupy your time in a productive way. Look for serving opportunities.

– You should not feel ashamed of receiving state unemployment payments. Contributions have been made to a fund for this very purpose.

– There is great blessing in belonging to a caring local church where practical and prayer support can be relied upon to see you through this time.

94

By following these guidelines and the other material in this lesson, you can prove yourself a man indeed, whatever your current job situation. May God bless you in it!

* *

LESSON 7

Something to Show: Work and productivity

True or False

1.   T F The need to work is all Adam's fault, a consequence of the Fall.

2.   T F For most Christians, fulfilment lies not in 'full time Christian service' but in doing their work as the will of God.

3.   T F As Christ's return approaches, the need to spend time in evangelism means that employment becomes unimportant.

4.   T F There will be work and responsibility in the age to come.

5.   T F Man is made to function best by taking one day's rest in seven.

6.   T F Biblical submission to our boss includes the right to express an opinion, question an attitude or voice a legitimate complaint.

7.   T F It is necessary to work specially hard when the boss is watching.

8.   T F The way a Christian man tackles his work can be a powerful aid to evangelism.

9.   T F Jealousy when a fellow-worker is promoted points to an attitude of self-interest which is out of place in a true man of God.

Group Discussion

1.   If you were an employer, what kind of attitudes would you most like to see in your workers?

2.   A man starts a new job which has a ten-minute mid-morning break as part of the agreement. On the first day, as he goes back to work after ten minutes, the other men say: 'Sit down; we know the break's supposed to be ten minutes but we always take at least twenty.' What, as a Christian man, should he do?

3.   In the light of this lesson, how should a man spend his time after retirement?

Personal Assignment

1.   Imagine your immediate boss giving to a friend an assessment of each of his workers. What do you think he would say about you? What strengths and weaknesses of yours as an employee would he highlight?

2.   Which of the world's attitudes to work have you unconsciously picked up? In the light of this lesson and your desire to be a man of God, list the practical changes you need to make. Start to put them into practice today!

True or False

1.F 2.T 3.F 4.T 5.T 6.T 7.F 8.T 9.T